The Volunteer Fundraiser's Handbook

The Volunteer Fundraiser's Handbook

Jimmy James

NELL JAMES PUBLISHERS

Published by Nell James Publishers
www.nelljames.co.uk
info@nelljames.co.uk

British Library Cataloguing-in-Publication Data
A catalogue record for this book is available from the British Library.

ISBN 978-0-9567024-8-7

First published 2014.

The Publisher has no responsibility for the persistence or accuracy of URLs for external or any third-party internet websites referred to in this book, and does not guarantee that any content on such websites is, or will remain, accurate or appropriate.

Note: The advice and information included in this book is published in good faith. However, the Publisher and author assume no responsibility or liability for any loss, injury or expense incurred as a result of relying on the information stated. Please check with the relevant persons and authorities regarding any legal and medical issues.

Printed in Great Britain.

Contents

Foreword 13

Preface... 15

Acknowledgements 17

Glossary 19

Chapter 1: Introducing charities 25

What is (a) charity?.. 25

Should your organisation become a charity or not? 26

How does your organisation become a charity?............. 28

What is a Governing Document?.................................... 30

Who are trustees? 30

Chapter 2: Starting your fundraising campaign 33

How did fundraising start?... 33

The principles of fundraising.. 34

Is your charity in good health? 34

Fundraising outside a campaign 35

Before your campaign starts 35

What is your project?.. 36

How much is your project going to cost?....................... 37

Making your campaign work...39

The Case Statement..41

The Case for Support..41

Financial programme 42

Checklist 43

Appendix A: BUSINESS PLANS...46

Appendix B: ORGANISATION OF THE CAMPAIGN
MANAGEMENT TEAM..50

Appendix C: CAMPAIGN MANAGEMENT TEAM – SAMPLE
TERMS OF REFERENCE 52

Appendix D: SAMPLE CAMPAIGN SECRETARY JOB
DESCRIPTION..54

Appendix E: CASE STATEMENT 57

Chapter 3: The preparation phase 61

The Fundraising Programme 61

Research..62

Training...66

Planning..66

Checklist 67

Appendix A: FUNDRAISING PROGRAMME 69

Chapter 4: First steps...73

Previous fundraising 73

Good housekeeping 73

Existing income 74

Tax efficient giving schemes 75

Use of facilities 76

Recycling 77

Checklist 79

Appendix A: HMRC and PAYROLL GIVING 81

Chapter 5: Trusts and foundations 85

Research tools 86

Trust application plan 88

Further research 90

Making your submission 91

Your application 91

Checklist 93

Appendix A: RESEARCHING GRANT-MAKING TRUSTS... 94

Appendix B: SAMPLE TRUST LETTER 99

Chapter 6: Statutory funds, the National Lottery and funds

from Europe 101

Statutory sources 102

National Government Statutory funds application plan..............103

Local Government statutory funds application plan....................104

The Landfill Communities Fund...106

The National Lottery 108

Funds from Europe 110

Checklist 112

Appendix A: DEMONSTRATING OUTCOMES.....................114

Chapter 7: Corporate donors 115

Why do companies give?..115

Aim...116

Which firms might give?...118

The List..118

Preparing 'The Ask'..119

Continuing relationships..120

Checklist 121

Chapter 8: Wealthy individuals 123

Celebrities and the 'Great & Good'...123

Initial research...124

Next steps..126

Checklist 127

Appendix A: EVALUATING INDIVIDUAL DONORS AND
OTHER KEY SUPPORTERS..129

Appendix B: ORGANISING A TRAINING SESSION...........133

Appendix C: UNDERTAKING A PERSONAL APPROACH
TO WEALTHY INDIVIDUALS..137

Appendix D (i): ORGANISING FUNDRAISING
RECEPTIONS..140

Appendix D (ii): FUNDRAISING RECEPTIONS SAMPLE
FOLLOW-UP LETTER..142

Chapter 9: Tax-efficient giving..143

Gift Aid...143

Covenants...145

Gifts of shares..146

Gifts of assets 146

Gifts-in-kind...147

Payroll Giving..147

Setting up a Payroll Giving Scheme..149

VAT 149

Appendix A: SAMPLE GIFT AID CERTIFICATE..................152

Appendix B: SAMPLE COVENANT...154

Chapter 10: Public relations..157

Stage One – Preparation..157

Stage 2 – Setting the scene 158

Stage 3 – Discussions with the media.............................159

Stage 4 – The PR Plan 160

Wider PR 162

Checklist 165

Appendix A: PUBLIC RELATIONS TRAINING 167

Appendix B: WEBSITE FUNDRAISING PAGES AIDE
MÉMOIRE 169

Chapter 11: Community fundraising 171

Organisation..172

Events 173

Sales..174

Community activities 175

Street collections..176

Lotteries and Raffles 176

Auctions..178

Recycling...178

On-line 180

Birthday, Christmas, wedding presents and funeral donations ...181

Challenge events 181

Crowdfunding 182

Checklist 182

Chapter 12: Support material 187

Brochures and leaflets 187

DVDs 190

Souvenirs 191

Checklist 192

Chapter 13: And finally … 193

Finale Event 193

Closing the Campaign Office 194

Checklist 195

Appendix A: LEGACY CAMPAIGNS – KEY POINTS 197

References 199

Professional bodies 199

Books/pamphlets 202

Websites 203

Index 207

Foreword

It gives me great pleasure to introduce this comprehensive handbook, the first of its kind aimed specifically at making fundraising accessible for non-professional, volunteer fundraisers. Volunteers and small charities are the backbone of the voluntary sector, but for charities and community groups without a dedicated fundraising team asking for money can seem complicated or, worse, embarrassing. Yet volunteer-led fundraising, from raffles to sponsored events to supermarket collections, raises a significant amount of revenue: in 2011/12, almost £3.5bn of the voluntary sector's income came from fundraising (National Council for Voluntary Organisations, 2014). Anything which makes this process easier and points charities towards useful resources and tips is, in my view, most welcome.

This book has come at an important time. Among the challenges of recent government cuts to the non-profit sector and increased competition for grants, charities must become more creative and look for funding in new places if they are to survive. For many charities, particularly small or volunteer-led organisations, raising much-needed revenue can be complex and time-consuming. This book comes with useful checklists, case studies, appendices and further sources of information to make fundraising as simple as possible for those who do it on a voluntary basis. Jimmy James' depth of experience as a professional fundraiser means his advice is practical, easy to follow and rooted in personal experience. I am sure this handbook will be a useful guide and reference point as you plan your own fundraising strategy.

The American author Cynthia Ozick wrote, 'We often take for granted the very things that most deserve our gratitude'. The publication of this book is an important step in recognising the wonderful contribution that volunteers make, on a daily basis and often in difficult circumstances, to deliver help and benefit to others. I hope this guide encourages you to go out and keep doing just that.

Sir Stuart Etherington
Chief Executive
National Council for Voluntary Organisations

Preface

The object of this book is to provide a concise and practical guide for small charities, community amateur sports clubs, charitable incorporated organisations and other voluntary groups on how to organise and run a fundraising campaign and how to raise funds in general.

It is aimed primarily at those charities which have no paid staff and which cannot afford the services of a fundraiser or fundraising consultant.

I have spent more of my working life in professional fundraising than in any other activity – and much of my free time as well engaged in voluntary charitable work. In partnership with volunteers and professionals in many fields, I have been able to raise millions of pounds for a wide variety of good causes throughout the United Kingdom and overseas.

In *The Volunteer Fundraiser's Handbook*, I have taken the reader through every stage of charity fundraising – from the setting up of a charity, through the planning and preparation of a fundraising campaign, followed by chapters dealing with all the major sources of funds a small charity might wish to access. I have also included chapters on tax-efficient giving, public relations, community fundraising and support material, concluding with recommendations for ensuring that a fundraising campaign that achieves its aims is not an end in itself, but the foundation for the charity's future success.

In recent years, I have been contacted by an increasing number of small charities and voluntary groups which seek professionals for their fundraising needs – but cannot afford to pay for them.

This book is for them.

JIMMY JAMES
Minerva Fundraising Consultancy
www.minervafundraising.com

Acknowledgements

During the course of writing this book, I have received a considerable amount of assistance and advice from individuals and institutions.

I wish to thank the following in particular for their invaluable help.

John Davey for his encouragement and wise advice about every aspect of this book.

Andrew Day, Group Chief Executive of Compton Fundraising Consultants Limited, and Paul Marvell, Director of Professional Development and Membership at the Institute of Fundraising for their detailed and helpful comments which resulted in significant changes to the book's contents.

Claire Rushton of John Wiley & Sons Limited; Teresa Scott and Adrian Warner of the National Council for Voluntary Organisations.

Finally, I wish to thank my wife for her tolerance and support throughout the time it has taken to complete this work.

JIMMY JAMES

Glossary

Advance Information Document (AID):
    See Special Prospects Document (SPD) below.

campaign brochure:
    A glossy campaigning publication, aimed at potential high level individual and corporate donors.

campaign leaflet:
    A low-level multi-use campaigning publication, usually in A4 tri-fold format.

Campaign Management Team (CMT):
    A group of individuals to whom the Trustees of a charity delegate the running of a fundraising campaign.

Campaign Secretary:
    Person appointed to oversee the administration of a fundraising campaign and to service its organisational parts.

Case Statement:
    A document outlining the rationale for a fundraising campaign.

Charitable Incorporated Organisations (CIO):
    Introduced in 2012. Registered with the Charity Commission but not with Companies House. Trustees have limited or no liability for CIOs' debts.

Charities Act(s):
    Acts of Parliament which define how charities are registered and regulated.

charity:
    Benevolence, especially to the poor; charitableness; alms-giving. In practice, a body registered as such with the Charity Commission for England and

Wales; the Office of the Scottish Charity Regulator; or The Charity Commission for Northern Ireland.

Charity Commission: The body which regulates charities in England and Wales. There is a separate Commission for Northern Ireland.

Chatham House Rule: When a meeting, or part thereof, is held under the Chatham House Rule, participants are free to use the information received, but neither the identity nor the affiliation of the speaker(s), nor that of any other participant, may be revealed. Frequently used in donor evaluation discussions.

chugging: Short for 'charity mugging', a slang description for the activities of paid fundraisers who stop people in the street to solicit charity donations.

Community Amateur Sports Clubs (CASCs):
Introduced in 2002, organisations registered as CASCs can benefit from a range of tax reliefs including Gift Aid, but are not registered charities.

Community Fundraising Team (CFT):
A group of individuals to whom the Trustees of a charity delegate the organisation and running of the community fundraising part of the charity's fundraising campaign.

Company Limited by Guarantee:
An alternative type of corporation used by charitable organisations that require legal personality.

constituency: A group of people or organisations likely to give to a charity. Subdivided into 'natural' and 'diffuse'. For example, the natural constituency of a school usually comprises the pupils; alumni/alumnae; current and past parents; Governing Body; staff. The diffuse constituency might be the village population served by the school which benefits from the school's facilities outside school hours.

covenant:
A legal document under which a donor agrees to gift a specific sum over a defined number of years through monthly, quarterly or annual payments. Largely superseded by Gift Aid.

crowdfunding:
A charity giving system where websites are set up which allow people or organisations to raise money for a project online through multiple donations or loans made by a number of donors over a short space of time. The best known such website in the UK is Peoplefund.it.

excepted charity:
A charity which does not have to register with the Charity Commission. The Commission is still responsible for its regulation.

exempted charity:
A charity which cannot register with the Charity Commission because it is regulated by another body.

empowerment funds:
Annual grants provided by some local councils to their elected councillors to enable them to fund charitable and other activities benefitting the residents of the Wards they represent.

Gift Aid:

Introduced in 1990. Allows charities (and CASCs) to reclaim the tax already paid on any sum given them at basic rate level. Allows higher rate taxpayers to reclaim the difference between the basic and higher rates on gifts they make to charities.

Giveacar:

A national charity fundraising scheme which allows owners of road legal and scrapped cars to give the cars' value to charity.

Governing Document:

A legal document which represents the rule book for the way in which the charity operates. Every charity must have one.

Grant-making Trusts (GMTs):

Charities whose sole purpose is to give funds to other charitable organisations. Also known as Foundations.

inoculation:

Process allowing a potential donor to give at well below their capacity, leading to him/her being 'inoculated' against future giving requests. Inoculation is usually the result of non-existent, or ill-planned, campaign management.

JustGiving:

An on-line and text charity donation scheme run by Vodafone.

Landfill Communities Fund (LCFs):

Set up in 1996 at the Landfill Tax Credit Scheme, the Fund enables landfill site operators to donate part of the taxes for which they are liable to defined charitable and other community projects.

MyDonate: A scheme similar to JustGiving, but run by British Telecom (BT).

Office of the Scottish Charity Regulator (OSCR):
                                The equivalent in Scotland of the Charity Commissions in England, Wales and Northern Ireland.

patron: A volunteer who may be a celebrity or other distinguished person who agrees to perform certain tasks on behalf of a charity. May be assisted by Vice Patrons. Sometimes known as a 'President'.

payroll giving: A national scheme whereby employees of a company can give regularly to a charity of their choice. Donations are deducted before tax.

Payroll Giving Agency (PGA):
                                An organisation which administers a Payroll Giving Scheme.

Special Prospects Document (SPD):
                                A working document used by the Campaign Management Team to raise major gifts in the early stages of a fundraising campaign. Also known as an Advance Information Document.

Statute of Charitable Uses:
                                First legal description of charity passed by Queen Elizabeth I in 1601. Superseded by Acts of Parliament passed since the Second World War.

statutory funds: Funds provided by the taxpayer through government sources at national, regional and local level.

taskforce: A sub-committee of the Campaign Management Team, given the responsibility of raising funds from a specific donor group.

tax-efficient giving: Schemes which allow charities and/or donors to benefit from HMRC charitable tax allowances.

The Sunday Times Rich List:

A list of the 1,000 wealthiest people or families in the United Kingdom published annually in April since 1989 by *The Sunday Times* newspaper.

trustees: Members of the governing body of a charity. May also be called 'directors', 'board members', 'governors' or 'committee members'.

Chapter 1: Introducing charities

What is (a) charity?

The word charity derives from the French *charité* and the Latin *caritas*. The word appears in the authorised and other versions of the Bible as a synonym for the love of God and man. The Oxford English Dictionary defines charity as 'benevolence, especially to the poor; charitableness; alms-giving.'

The first legal description of charity appears in the Statute of Charitable Uses, passed by Queen Elizabeth I in 1601. The pre-amble to the Statute states that the following activities are charitable:

Relief of the aged, impotent, and poor people; maintenance of sick and maimed soldiers and mariners; schools of learning; free schools and scholars in universities; repair of bridges, ports, havens, causeways, churches, seabanks, and highways; education and preferment of orphans; the relief, stock, or maintenance of houses of correction; marriages of poor maids; support, aid, and help of young tradesmen, handicraftsmen and persons decayed; relief or redemption of prisoners or captives; and the aid or ease of any poor inhabitants covering payments of fifteens, setting out of soldiers, and other taxes.

Despite the fact that this definition of charitable activities is now over 400 years old, many of the examples still hold good today. More importantly, the Statute of Charitable Uses set down clearly a basic principle of the United Kingdom's outlook on charitable giving over many years, namely that it exists for those who are well off to help provide opportunities for those who are not.

If we understand the history of charitable giving and what it has achieved in our country, we are better able participate in, and donate to, today's charities – and persuade others to do likewise.

The Statute's definition remained the benchmark for assessing charitable status until the after the Second World War when a number of Acts of Parliament were passed. The principal of these were:

- Charities Act 1960: This established the central register of charities (maintained by the Charity Commission for England and Wales);
- Charities Act 1992;
- Charities Act 2006;
- Charities and Trustee Investment (Scotland) Act 2005 This established the Office of the Scottish Charity Regulator (OSCR), the Scottish equivalent of the Charity Commission for England and Wales;
- The Charities Act (Northern Ireland) 2008, which set in place the Charity Commission for Northern Ireland (CCNI). The CCNI started to register charities on 16 December 2013.

The most important Act at the time of writing is The Charities Act 2011, which came into effect on 14 March 2012. It is the Act of Parliament which sets out how all charities in England and Wales are registered and regulated.

It replaces:

- Most of the Charities Acts 1992, 1993 and 2006;
- All of the Recreational Charities Act 1958.

It does not replace the sections in earlier Charities Acts about fundraising which haven't taken effect yet, for example, charitable collections in public places.

Should your organisation become a charity or not?

There are inevitably pros and cons to becoming a charity.

- Charities can fundraise more widely. Some organisations, for example grant-making trusts, will only donate to registered charities. Many other donors – individual and corporate – will also exclude organisations which are not charities because charity registration provides some guarantees that the organisation is sustainable and that donated funds will be used as the donor has laid down;

- Lack of charity registration is no bar to receiving local government grants, awards from the National Lottery or funds from the European Union;
- A voluntary or community organisation which is not a charity avoids the Charity Commission's requirements in terms of registration and annual reporting, and it can still carry on work in the community similar to that of a charity;
- A registered charity must obey the Charity Commission's regulations and cannot become involved in political activity.

Many charities are also registered as Companies Limited by Guarantee (CLGs). This is an alternative form of corporation used by non-profit organisations which require legal personality. Many clubs and membership organisations are CLGs. CLGs may additionally convert to charitable status, so long as their articles of incorporation prevent the distribution of any profits to members.

Since the beginning of the century, the Government announced two new organisations which are alternatives to that of registered charity:

- Community Amateur Sports Clubs (CASCs). This category was introduced in 2002, and allows amateur sports clubs to register with HMRC and benefit from a range of tax reliefs including Gift Aid. CASCs must meet a number of requirements, the principal of these being the need to provide facilities for one or more sports deemed to be eligible under the scheme; and the need to encourage participation in the sport(s) concerned. As CASCs are not registered charities, they may be liable to corporation tax on all or some of their profits;
- Charitable Incorporated Organisations (CIOs). This category was introduced in 2012. A CIO is an incorporated form of charity which is registered with the Charity Commis-

sion but not with Companies House. It can enter into contracts in its own right and its trustees will normally have limited or no liability for the debts of the CIO.

Before coming to a decision, it is wise to seek advice as to the best way forward for your particular organisation. The Institute of Fundraising – www.institute-of-fundraising.org.uk – provides a wealth of information and advice on this and every other area connected with fundraising and charitable giving.

How does your organisation become a charity?

If you believe that your organisation's activities are charitable and you wish to register as a charity, you can apply to the Charity Commission for England and Wales; the Office of the Scottish Charity Regulator; or the Charity Commission for Northern Ireland, as appropriate. The steps you will need to take to register are as follows:

• You must establish your charitable purposes. Eligible purposes are set out in the Charities Act 2011;

• Your charity must meet the Public Benefit requirement. Under the Statute of Charitable Uses 1601, certain activities were deemed to be charitable *per se*. This is no longer the case, and an organisation wishing to register as a charity needs to be able to show public benefit;

• The charity must have a suitable 'Governing document'. This is a document setting out the charity's purposes and, usually, how it is to be administered. It may be a trust deed, constitution, articles of association, will, conveyance, Royal Charter, Scheme of the Commission, or other formal document;

• The charity must have trustees who are jointly responsible for the running of the charity. Trustees are the people who serve on the governing body of a charity. They may be known as trustees, directors, board members, governors or committee members. Charity trustees are responsible for the general control and management of the administration of a

charity. The great majority serve as volunteers and receive no payment for their work;
• The charity will need a bank account.

The registration process takes about 30 days. The Charity Commission does not charge a fee for charity registration. Further details and guidance are available on the following websites:
• England and Wales: www.charitycommission.gov.uk
• Scotland: www.oscr.org.uk
• Northern Ireland: www.charitycommissionni.org.uk

Confusingly, it may not actually be necessary for your organisation to register in order to become a charity. It will not have to register if it falls into any of the following categories, although it will of course still have to have charitable purposes (see above):
• Its annual income is less than £25,000;
• Its Head Office isn't in the country where it is operating;
• It is part of a larger organisation or charity;
• It is 'excepted' from registration. 'Except' means that the Charity Commission is responsible for its regulation but there is no requirement for it to register. 'Excepted' charities include churches of certain Christian denominations; and Scout and Guide groups;
• It is 'exempted' from registration. 'Exempt' means that the charity cannot register with the Charity Commission because they are regulated by another body. Exempted charities include most universities in England and many national museums and galleries.

The procedure if your organisation wishes to register as a charity is set out in detail on the Charity commission website.

What is a Governing Document?

A Governing Document is a legal document which represents the rule book for the way in which a charity operates. It should contain information about:

- What the charity is set up to do (its aims, 'objects' or 'purposes');
- How the charity will do those things (powers);
- Who will run it (charity trustees);
- What happens if changes to the administrative provisions need to be made (amendment provision);
- What happens if the charity wishes to wind up (dissolution provision).

It should also contain the following administrative provisions:

- How the charity trustees will run it;
- Internal arrangements for meetings, voting, looking after money, etc.

A sample Governing Document is available on the Charity Commission website.

Who are trustees?

Charity trustees:

- Are the people who form the governing body or 'board' of a charity;
- May be called trustees, directors, board members, governors or committee members;
- Are the people with ultimate responsibility for directing the business of the charity;
- Are mostly volunteers, and receive no payment (except out-of-pocket expenses) – although the Government is considering making changes to this.

Trustees are responsible for:

- Making the decisions about the charity's finances, activities and plans for the future;
- Giving leadership and direction;
- Employing staff;
- Developing the skills they need to be effective in their role;
- Preparing for and attending trustee meetings.

Recruitment of trustees can be achieved through:
- Placing advertisements in the general or charity press;
- Using specialist organisations such as Trustees Unlimited which specialise in finding charity trustees;
- Radio appeals;
- Word-of-mouth.

It is essential that a Board of Trustees is not just a group of friends or business colleagues, but contains people with a range of skills, including:
- Financial;
- Legal;
- Human Resources;
- Fundraising.

It is also wise to recruit a reasonable balance of people of different sexes and from different religious, social and ethnic backgrounds including people with disabilities. In addition, it is helpful to have as wide a range of ages as possible so that the Board reflect diverse viewpoints and a mix of youthful energy and the experience which comes with age.

Above all, trustees must not only be enthusiastic for the charity's cause, but they must be briefed on what is expected of them; not simply what is required by the Charity Commission but also any other activities expected of them, for example participation in fundraising and personal giving to the charity.

Trustees need to be recruited before you apply to be a registered charity.

Chapter 2: Starting your fundraising campaign

How did fundraising start?

No one knows exactly when the first fundraising campaign took place, but charity fundraising has been with us for many years. In 1180, Prior Benedict became Abbot of Peterborough. On arrival he discovered that the finances of the Abbey (now Peterborough Cathedral) were in a parlous state with a constant annual deficit and no funds to pay for urgently needed repairs.

Benedict had witnessed the murder of Thomas à Becket at Canterbury Cathedral in 1170. Accordingly, he returned briefly to Canterbury where he obtained a piece of the cloak Becket was wearing when he was murdered, together with a phial of his blood. On his return to Peterborough, he charged visitors to the Abbey 1d to touch the piece of cloak and to drink a glass of water to which one drop of blood had been added. Within a year, the Abbey's finances had been restored, and the repair work paid for and in progress – and miraculously the phial of blood had not run out (or so they say!).

For much of the 20th century, fundraising was an amateur pastime where the Women's Institute and other groups sold jam and cakes or organised jumble sales, and a few hardy souls braved the elements to shake a tin outside the local supermarket.

Today it is a multi-million pound business operation, led by teams of professionals. The legacy market alone in the UK was worth some £1.94 billion in 2008.

On the other hand there are tens of thousands of small charities which need to raise funds but cannot afford professional assistance. If you are involved in one of these, where do you start?

The principles of fundraising

Throughout your fundraising campaign and the plans you will be making for it, you will have much to consider. But you should always keep at the back of your mind the 4 Principles of Fundraising. These are:

- There must be a persuasive case. No one follows an uncertain trumpet and no one gives to a charity or project unless they are persuaded that it merits their support;

- There must be a detailed financial programme. Today, potential donors will need to be convinced that you have got your sums right; that your project will be sustainable and not prove to be a white elephant. Everyone remembers the Millennium Dome!

- There must be an identifiable constituency. 'Constituency' in fundraising is the word used to describe the people who might give to a charitable project. The constituency is divided between 'natural' and 'diffuse'. So, for example, if you are a primary school raising funds for a new hall and indoor play area, your natural constituency will be those most intimately involved and those who stand to benefit most, i.e. governors, staff and parents of children in the school. Your diffuse constituency will be former parents (who will have a warm glow towards the school for what it provided for their children) and members of your village or local community who will see the school improving and may well have the opportunity to use the new facilities outside school hours;

- There must be active, influential volunteer leadership. This is especially important in a small charity where there are no, or minimal, paid staff and where you cannot afford to retain a fundraising consultant or take a fundraiser onto your payroll.

Is your charity in good health?

Visitors to Peterborough may have been prepared to give money to the Abbey at Benedict's request on the basis that he was a senior clergyman and the Church was held in more reverence than it is today. But Benedict also suggested that spiritual and physical benefit would follow touching the piece of Becket's cloak and drinking water mingled with his blood. The visitors clearly overlooked the poor financial governance at the Abbey before Benedict's arrival in their desire to receive the perceived benefits they would gain for donating 1d.

Today people are more demanding and potential funders will want assurance that your charity is properly administered and that their donations will not be wasted.

Fundraising outside a campaign

This book is aimed primarily at small charities that need to raise funds for a particular capital item or project, and have neither the experience to mount a campaign themselves, nor the funds to buy-in professional expertise.

However, some small charities will simply need to raise money for their core activities and ensure that their beneficiaries continue to receive the services they provide.

For these charities, there will be no need for a 'campaign' as such. Nonetheless, there will still be a requirement for a fundraising programme within the overall business plan, and the need for teams of volunteers to organise continuous fundraising across the board to meet their charity's targets. Moreover, there will still be a need to involve high profile local people, establish relationships with trusts and foundations which support charities in their particular county or unitary authority, and encourage supporters to give on a regular basis.

Before your campaign starts

So before you start planning your fundraising campaign, your charity needs to have:
- A report and set of accounts for the previous twelve month period. This document must be produced irrespective of the size of your charity, and also if you are a CIO. If your

charity's annual income does not exceed £25,000 or if you are an excepted charity, you do not need to file the report and accounts with the Charity Commission and the accounts needed to be inspected rather than audited. Full details of charity accounting requirements are set out in the Charity Commission's website www.charity-commission.gov.uk;

•   A business plan. This will not only explain your charity's aims and how the money you are requesting will be spent, but it will also give potential donors confidence that the charity has got its act together. Your business plan needs to be detailed and realistic and carefully costed before you start fundraising. Your fundraising campaign will not be an operation in itself – it will underpin the business plan. If none of your volunteers has written a business plan before, co-opt an outsider who has done so and ask them to check yours over and make sure it all adds up. Finally, your Business Plan needs to have the endorsement of your Trustees and other key volunteers. If they are not 100% behind the Business Plan, they are unlikely to give your fundraising campaign the support it will require for its success. You will find a Business Plan *aide mémoire* at Appendix A to this chapter.

What is your project?

Fundraising is a business operation and needs to be approached in a business-like way. You need to understand this, because that is how most of your potential donors will see it. You – and they – would not dream of investing in a company without studying its accounts, checking on its suppliers and clients, investigating its cash flow and looking at its products or services.

So you need to be clear that you are not simply fundraising for your charity's objects in general – you are fundraising for something specific that you can explain to potential donors, even if that 'specific' is simply to increase your annual income so that you can do your core work more effectively.

Your trustees and volunteers need to decide exactly what it is the charity wants to raise funds for - and then stick to this.

How much is your project going to cost?

The short answer is – no one can be sure until it is complete! However, your potential supporters and funders will need to see that you have at least taken reasonable steps to cost your campaign objectives.

Revenue

If your fundraising campaign is being planned to increase your charity's annual income, then you will need to explain:

- Why a sudden increase has become necessary?
- Steps you have taken to reduce the charity's costs so that this extra sum is kept to a minimum. Such steps could include putting out service contracts to re-tender; comparing consumables suppliers with their competitors; and ensuring that maximum use is made of tax efficient schemes such as Gift Aid;
- The advantages to the charity's beneficiaries and to the wider community that the increased funds will bring.

Project

If your campaign's aim is to raise funds for a specific project – which could, for example, involve recruitment of a new staff member – you will need to show that:

- The project is necessary now when it was not previously;
- The benefits which the project will bring;
- How the project will be sustained once the funds raised for setting it up have been exhausted, e.g. by charging for the services the project will provide.

Capital

Whether your campaign is to raise funds to build a new building or repair an existing one, or to purchase an item or items of equipment, you will need to show:

- Evidence that the published cost is realistic. For equipment, this could be based on three quotes from different

37

suppliers. For a building, this will be based on estimates from an architect, surveyor or structural engineer: it is unlikely that you will have put out a capital project to tender before at least a proportion of the funds necessary have been raised;

• A clear indication of what aspects of the project are subject to VAT – and the sum involved;

• Your plans – if any – to seek gifts 'in kind' to reduce the campaign target figure;

• The inclusion of a realistic contingency fund against price and fee increases and unforeseen costs which only become apparent when the project is underway (this is particularly true of repairs to existing buildings and restoration of artefacts).

Costing your project

Costing your project can be a vicious circle, particularly if you are seeking to raise funds initially so that you can undertake the investigations on say, a listed building, which are necessary before you can determine what work needs doing and thus what needs to be costed in the first place. A good way to proceed involves the following steps:

• Find out what grants may be available for the investigations required;

• Approach funders and ask what they will fund in terms of investigations; whether they will fund work which has taken place, or not; and whether there are any caveats, e.g. that investigating persons or bodies need to have specific qualifications or accreditation;

• Once you have received grant money for investigations, appoint an architect, surveyor or structural engineer as appropriate to carry out the investigative work. Ensure that he/she/they include estimated costs of any work they propose you should undertake.

Once you have the estimate, this will not only allow you to fix a campaign target but will also enable you to benchmark the estimate against contractors' quotes when you eventually put the project out to tender.

Making your campaign work

If your charity does not fundraise on a regular basis, it probably won't have the administrative and support elements in place which are necessary for a successful campaign.

First, you will need people.

You will need a group of individuals who are going to run the campaign and make the key decisions about it. These could be your trustees, other volunteer supporters – or a mix of both. This team or committee will need a leader, a Treasurer and a Secretary, at the least. We'll call this grouping the Campaign Management Team (CMT).You will find a sample organisation for a CMT at Appendix B to this chapter.

You will then need to decide the size of the CMT and what its Terms of Reference (TsOR) will be. This is important, as it will report to the trustees and its leader will need to know, in particular, which decisions the CMT is empowered to take and which should be referred to the trustees for their decision. A sample TsOR can be found at Appendix C to this chapter.

Next, is the CMT going to manage all aspects of the campaign, or are there going to be small sub-committees, which we will call taskforces? There might, for example, be a taskforce for seeking individual gifts; a taskforce for corporate gifts; and a taskforce for community fundraising (see p.171). The advantages of creating taskforces are that they involve more people to the campaign; they take work away from the CMT and allow the latter to concentrate on high-level decision-making; and they involve volunteers in specific roles where their talents may be particularly beneficial to the campaign. However, many charities will find that they have insufficient volunteers to man these taskforces or insufficient volunteers of a high enough calibre. In these cases, the taskforces will create work for the CMT, rather than reduce it, because they are not capable of fulfilling their roles and these then have to be taken over by the CMT.

The campaign, including the CMT, will need a volunteer secretary or administrator. This ideally will be a retired person who has held a senior PA role in their working life. The importance of having a campaign secretary cannot be over-emphasised, because potential donors and supporters need a point-of-contact through the working day. Whilst voicemail has an important role, voicemail messages which remain unanswered for days at a time are not likely to create support for the campaign, and will convey a lack of professionalism. The CMT, for example, will typically consist of busy people who are happy to give up some of their time to be a member of the CMT and help to carry out its role. These people will, understandably, expect support for the quality time they are giving up, and this support will include timely meeting agendas and minutes, briefing notes and other information. When they go about bringing in gifts to the campaign, they will expect support in the form of briefing packs, thank-you letters and other items. It is both unrealistic and inefficient to expect a number of different volunteers to carry out this role, so the appointment of a Campaign Secretary at an early stage in the campaign is critical. A sample job description for Campaign Secretary can found at Appendix D to this chapter.

Secondly, you will need facilities. Your newly appointed Campaign Secretary will need somewhere to work which will act as the hub of the fundraising campaign. Whilst the use of a room in a volunteer's house can work successfully, a Campaign Office in a more public place such as a village hall or in a company office room loaned by a local business is generally more effective.

The Campaign Office will need to be properly equipped: computer, printer, telephone with voicemail and filing cabinet as a minimum. Whilst it makes sound sense to acquire second hand chairs and filing cabinets, donated elderly computers with long-past versions of Microsoft are a false economy. The campaign is a business operation – and needs effective equipment to support it.

The CMT will also require a place to meet and where volunteers can brief potential donors and new volunteers. Again, the concept of meeting in a CMT member's house has economic advantages, but a Campaign Office which is large enough to double as a small conference room, or which has a meeting room nearby, is preferable.

The Case Statement

No one will follow an uncertain trumpet, so if you are serious about fundraising, your campaign will need a Case Statement. This document, around 1–1.5 sides of A4 paper, spells out clearly the rationale for your campaign – what you need to raise funds for and why. It is critical that time and effort are spent in getting this right, for it should form the basis of all subsequent fundraising literature and other fundraising and publicity aids. The Case Statement should be formally adopted by the CMT and approved by the Trustees.

The Case Statement should make clear:
- The reasons for the fundraising campaign;
- The fundraising projects and objectives;
- The ultimate beneficiaries of the campaign which may go beyond those normally associated with the charity's work;
- The public benefit which will result from the campaign.

The Case Statement is not for external use, but it will serve as the basis for the campaign's fundraising literature, including applications for grants. An example of a Case Statement can be found at Appendix E to this chapter.

The Case for Support

The Case Statement is a concise document aimed at concentrating the minds of your Trustees and the CMT. If your fundraising campaign is a large one, or if it has multiple projects or complex aims, it may be necessary to develop the Case Statement into a longer and more detailed document – the Case for Support.

The Case for Support will form the basis of the Special Prospects Document (see p.189), and will include the following:

- Your trustees' vision for the charity as a whole and the aims of, and need for, a fundraising campaign in particular;
- The feasibility study carried out (if any) and the options considered before the campaign projects were decided;
- The arguments necessary to persuade different groups of potential donors to support the campaign;
- A market analysis, including identification of the campaign's 'constituency', and a SWOT (strengths, weaknesses, opportunities, threats) analysis;
- The campaign structure, including the background and roles of the campaign leaders.

Financial programme

People have long memories and in the last 20 years there have been some notable instances of charitable projects that have soaked up large sums of public and private money with limited positive results.

Your financial programme will be covered by the Finance section of your Business Plan, but it will need updates. Whereas the Business Plan as a whole will be written for five to ten years ahead, the financial programme will need more frequent updating, particularly if no fundraising campaign was envisaged at the time the Business Plan was written. Common causes for financial programme updating include:

- Your project has changed;
- The timeframe for your project has changed;
- Your campaign is progressing faster or slower than you had anticipated.

So the financial programme must address the following:

- Can all the aims of the fundraising campaign be justified?
- Have all reasonable contingencies been allowed for?
- How does the campaign's financial programme relate to the charity's overall funding policy?
- Is the project or projects for which the campaign seeks to raise funds likely to be attractive to potential donors?

Your financial programme is for both internal and external use, as is the Business Plan of which it is a part. Internally it will assure your Trustees, volunteers and existing supporters (e.g. *Friends*) that you have costed the projects accurately and produced a budget for the campaign which is both realistic and convincing. Externally it will stand up to the closest scrutiny of potential donors whose funds will be limited and who will want the reassurance that an effective financial programme will provide.

Once these matters have been effectively addressed, you will be able to start the preparation phase for the fundraising campaign itself. But before you do so, ensure that you have visited the websites of the following:
- The Institute of Fundraising: www.institute-of-fundraising.org.uk
- The Fundraising Standards Board: www.frsb.org.uk

In particular, close attention should be paid to the IoF's Code of Practice and the Standards section of the FRSB's website. Following these will ensure that your campaign is ethical and legal as well as successful!

Checklist

Project
- What is the project?
- Project agreed by trustees;
- Project costed.

Documentation
- Business Plan produced/updated. Professionally checked;
- Business plan agreed by Trustees and other key volunteers;
- Financial programme within Business Plan supports fundraising campaign;
- Annual report and accounts for last two years available and audited/inspected.

Campaign people
- Campaign Management Team recruited;
- Chairman appointed;
- Other key roles appointed;
- Team's TsOR agreed by Trustees;
- Taskforces recruited;
- Campaign Secretary/administrator recruited;
- Roles defined and agreed by Trustees/CMT.

Campaign facilities
- Campaign Office located;
- Meeting facilities in Campaign Office or nearby;
- Campaign Office equipment agreed and purchased/donated.

Case Statement
- Case Statement drafted;
- Contains key information;
- Adopted by CMT;
- Approved by trustees.

Case for Support
- Need for Case for Support;
- Key elements included;
- Approved by Trustees.

Financial programme
- Updated within Business Plan;
- Supports aims of campaign;
- Covers contingency costs;
- Dovetails in with charity's overall funding policies.

Appendix A: BUSINESS PLANS

Why a business plan?
A charity produces a business plan to demonstrate that:
- It takes a realistic view of its current position;
- Its trustees and management know where it is going;
- Its trustees and management have carefully considered options and requirements for future development.

The business plan provides trustees and management with a roadmap for action and a yardstick against which to measure progress. It can also be used as a key communication tool to highlight strategy and direction within a charity and to elicit the confidence and support of existing and potential future funders.

The plan typically makes projections for five to ten years in the future and should cover the following elements:
- Operations: this will include the day-to-day running of the charity; key processes; resource needs; Governance; location and risk management issues;
- Finance: an assessment of fixed and variable costs and minimum financial requirements. It should include a detailed cashflow forecast and also a financial programme for any fundraising campaign to be undertaken during the life of the Business Plan;
- Fundraising and Public Relations (PR): an outline of how the fundraising effort is going to support the charity's operations, and in particular how it will bridge the gap between the charity's needs and the income it derives from other established sources, e.g. Service Level Agreements (SLAs) or trading operations. In addition, an outline of the PR strategy and how that will support and dovetail in with the fundraising campaign;
- Human resources: including recruitment, retention, compensation and leadership of the charity.

Before starting to write the business plan, it is useful to carry out the following:

• A SWOT analysis (strengths, weaknesses, opportunities, threats). This is particularly important when a fundraising campaign is planned as it will identify in particular how the charity is perceived by the public at large in the area where it operates, and what competition a campaign is likely to meet from other charities fundraising locally;

• A PEST analysis (political, economic, social and technological) which will give the Business Plan a broad perspective of the potential influences and factors likely to affect the charity. The failure of many charities to undertake a PEST analysis in the first decade of the 21st century led to numbers facing funding crises when statutory grants were reduced and SLAs cancelled.

The key areas which a charity's Business Plan should cover are as follows:

The context

• The charity's background, its objects and the services it provides;

• The client group and the geographical area in which it operates;

• Past and current performance;

• Key factors that might affect the success or failure of the charity's services;

• The skills and experience of the Trustees, management team and other key volunteers.

Define objectives

• Short term targets;

• Longer term targets;

• Identify key performance indicators (KPIs);

• Consider use of SMART objectives (specific, measurable, agreed, realistic, time-bound);

• Include contingency plan if objectives are not reached.

Perform market analysis:
- Your analysis will need to convince readers that there is a demand for your charity's services; that you know who your client group is; and that you understand what changes are affecting the marketplace where you are working;
- Include a brief overview of the charity sector with particular reference to the segment where you are working;
- Give detailed information on your current and potential future client group;
- Charities or private/public sector organisations which offer the same or similar services in the area where your charity operates;
- Factors which currently affect the delivery of your charity's services, or may affect it in the future. These might include economic trends, legislation, social factors and demographic changes.

The charity's plans for
- Operations;
- Finance, including a financial programme for any planned fundraising campaign(s);
- Fundraising and PR;
- Human resources.

Conclude with the key message
- Strategic direction;
- Strengths;
- Unique features and benefits;
- Proposed timetable of events to demonstrate sound planning;
- Provide appropriate appendices to give the plan additional information and data.

Provide an Executive Summary

- This is arguably the most important element of the plan as it appears at the front and will be read before anything else;
- It must engage the reader's interest and clearly set out the Business Plan's contents;
- It must convince the reader not only that the trustees and management team understand the charity's business proposition, but also that they have clearly identified how to manage the requirements and risks going forward;
- The summary should at the least make mention of any planned fundraising campaign(s).

Appendix B: ORGANISATION OF THE CAMPAIGN MANAGEMENT TEAM

The Campaign Management Team (CMT) will vary in its organisation dependent upon the nature and size of the fundraising campaign and the element of full-time management in the charity, if any. A CMT will typically consist of 7 people:

Chairman

This person will be a senior volunteer within the charity who is dedicated to the charity's objects; has wide experience of business operations in general and those of the charity in particular; and has the time and energy to take on the role. He/she will probably be a longstanding trustee of the charity, but not the Chairman of trustees.

Treasurer

The Treasurer should have some relevant qualification and experience in accounting – ideally a Chartered Accountant. He/she should be completely conversant with charity accounting in particular, or prepared to become so before the campaign is initiated.

Public Relations representative

This person should be employed in, or recently retired from, either the PR industry or the media. Failing the availability of anyone from these categories, an enthusiastic person with marketing experience should be recruited (see p.156).

Major gifts representative

Gifts from wealthy individuals in the charity's catchment area are likely to be an important part of the fundraising campaign. A person with extensive contacts, professionally and/or socially with those who are both likely to be sympathetic to the charity's cause and also able to make substantial gifts, will enhance the chances of the campaign's success. Ideally this person should

also have the business contacts to bring on board corporate donors.

Research leader

The researching of grant-making trusts and businesses likely to
support the fundraising campaign will be critical to its success.
Without detailed research, much time, effort and money will be
wasted. The research leader should be prepared to undertake key
research himself/herself, but also to recruit other volunteers
connected with the charity to help undertake the research tasks
necessary (see p.62).

Community fundraising representative

The ultimate success of any fundraising campaign will depend
on much wider support than is provided by the charity Trustees,
management and existing volunteers. Members of the community at large should be encouraged to organise fundraising activities in support of the campaign as well as giving to it.
Community organisations and groups will need to be briefed;
offered suggestions about fundraising activities; and assisted in
organising the activities. The community fundraising representative will be a natural and enthusiastic organiser who will lead this
aspect of the campaign (see p.171).

Campaign Secretary

See Annex D to this chapter for Campaign Secretary Job Description (p.54).

Appendix C: CAMPAIGN MANAGEMENT TEAM – SAMPLE TERMS OF REFERENCE

Membership
• The Campaign Management Team (CMT) shall be appointed by the Board of Trustees and shall consist of a Chairman (who shall be a Trustee); Treasurer; Research leader; representatives for PR and for major gifts; the Campaign Secretary; and such additional members as the Chairman may see fit to appoint in consultation with the Board of Trustees;
• A quorum shall be 4 members.

Frequency of meetings
• The CMT will meet not less than once a month during the fundraising campaign and at such other times as the Chairman may require;
• A meeting of the CMT may be called by any member of the team.

Duties
• To lead and organise the fundraising campaign in accordance with the instructions set out by the Board of Trustees;
• To ensure that the fundraising campaign is pursued in accordance with the objects of the charity;
• To ensure financial probity and competence in all aspects of fundraising;
• To co-opt such extra personnel and to delegate to them such tasks as it considers appropriate for the effective running of the campaign and the achievement of its target(s).

Reporting procedures
• The Chairman of the CMT shall report to the Board of Trustees on the progress of the campaign in general and on matters dealt with by the CMT in particular at the next meeting of the Board following the relevant CMT meeting;

• Minutes of all CMT meetings are to be circulated to the Board and a summary posted on the charity's website.

Appendix D: SAMPLE CAMPAIGN SECRETARY JOB DESCRIPTION

The Trustees of XYZ Charity seek a responsible, flexible, full-time (part-time) person for the position of Campaign Secretary for their planned fundraising campaign.

Responsibilities
The Campaign Secretary will, under the direction of the Chairman of the Campaign Management Team (CMT), be responsible for the day-to-day running of the Campaign Office. This will include:
- Recording all donations;
- Maintenance of records of names and addresses of donors;
- Thanking donors;
- Word-processing letters;
- Maintaining records of campaign expenses and petty cash;
- Dealing with members of the public and visitors to the Campaign Office;
- Maintaining proper records of stocks of campaign literature and publicity material.

The Secretary will be numerate and literate and have a good telephone manner. Word processing skills are essential, as well as a good working knowledge of Microsoft Word and Access. Previous PA experience together with shorthand and audio capabilities is desirable. An ability to relate to people at all levels will be a distinct advantage. From time to time it may be necessary for the Campaign Secretary to work in the evening or at week-ends. A clean driving licence and car are desirable.

General duties
- Be responsible for the daily routine of the Campaign Office, serving the CMT and any other volunteer groups set up for the campaign, and monitoring their activities;

- Maintain records of all actual and prospective donors and other contacts. To research additional sources as briefed, including making personal contact with the correspondents of grant-making trusts;
- Maintain all records of expenditure, including petty cash;
- Order necessary stationery and office supplies subject to agreed authorisation limits;
- Deal with all visitors to the Campaign Office in an appropriate manner;
- Liaise with Campaign PR representative to ensure a regular flow of campaign publicity;
- Liaise with the Campaign Treasurer to ensure that financial records of income and expenditure are maintained; gifts and grants are banked in a timely manner; and appropriate returns are made to HMRC and claims for Gift Aid submitted;
- Carry out all such other duties as may be determined from time to time by the CMT Chairman.

Secretarial Duties
- Act as PA to the Chairman of the CMT;
- Answer the telephone and ensure a voicemail service is set up outside normal working hours;
- Arrange meetings and be responsible for the organisation of the CMT Chairman's diary;
- Arrange for major donations to be suitably acknowledged, and personally thank smaller donors.

Maintenance of records
- Maintain the record of donations on a daily basis;
- Maintain records of all payments by covenant and Gift Aid in the agreed format;
- Maintain records of appeal expenses under budget headings and report monthly to the CMT Chairman;
- Maintain petty cash book;

- Be responsible for all filing of correspondence, minutes of meetings etc.

Working arrangements
The position is based at....................

Details of hours worked will be discussed. Initially a 35 hour (or 17.5 hour) week is proposed, times to be arranged to suit the secretary and the CMT Chairman.

An honorarium of £.......... is offered (if post is not voluntary) for a 12 month fixed term, and agreed expenses will be paid.

Appendix E: CASE STATEMENT

The Case Statement is an essential part of any fundraising campaign. Not only does it allow trustees and the Campaign Management Team to establish the rationale for the campaign, but it also serves as the basis for subsequent campaign literature such as brochures, leaflets, website pages and submission letters to potential funders.

The following Case Statement example is from an actual fundraising campaign:

***

Littlevillage Guildhall is a 15th Century Grade 1 listed community building owned by the Littlevillage Guildhall Trust (registered charity no 123456).

The Guildhall was built by the Guild of the Holy Trinity in around 1450. The role of the Guild was to pay for a Guild priest who was responsible for the spiritual welfare of Guild members and for educating local boys in Latin grammar. The Guildhall would have been used as a community centre, in particular as a fundraising venue to support the Guild's activities.

Social changes in the 16th century saw a dramatic reduction in the role of Guilds with the result that the Littlevillage Guildhall became derelict.

In the mid-17th Century, the local landowner Sir Rich Manne had the building restored and then sold it to the village for £50 (about £6,000 in 21st century terms) for use as either a school or almshouses. Whilst its use as a school gradually died out over the centuries, almshouses were a feature of Littlevillage Guildhall until the mid-1920s.

By the late 1940s, the Guildhall had fallen into disrepair, but thanks to a fundraising campaign started in 1948, restoration work was undertaken and completed in 1961.

Littlevillage Guildhall is only one of very few timber-frame Guildhalls left in the United Kingdom. An estimated 15,000 visitors a year from all over the UK and overseas come to visit Littlevillage, and the Guildhall is one of the oldest secular buildings in the parish and one of the village's star attractions.

By 2001, some 40 years' after the restoration project, the Guildhall was again in a poor state of repair and unable to fulfil its function either in providing almshouses to a standard acceptable in the 21st century or to offer the community in Littlevillage and the surrounding area an effective meeting place.

While the work done between 1948 and 1961 has been a vital factor in preserving the building, modern conservation practices, endorsed by English Heritage, mean that we can carry out the project using similar materials and techniques to those used when it was first built.

Unfortunately these 15th century techniques and materials are now seen as incompatible with much of those used in the 1950s. This means most of the building will need to be stripped down to its timber skeleton.

Accordingly, a project plan has been set in place to restore the Guildhall to its original state, whilst at the same time providing the residents of Littlevillage with a practical and multi-purpose community facility. The restoration project will involve:

- Stripping out the cement render, concrete walls and modern partitions from the 1950s;
- Repairing the oak frame and roof timbers and restoring the roof, using as many of the existing roof tiles as possible;
- Coating the wall with traditional lime render, repairing the original wattle and daub, and replacing concrete floors with limecrete and brick;
- Installing insulation and heating systems which are sympathetic to the construction of the original building;
- Installing a kitchen, WCs, new staircase and pneumatic lift to allow access for able-bodied people and those with disabilities to both floors;
- Re-ordering the internal layout to provide a Library, Museum and community venue for meetings, exhibitions, performances and functions.

The cost of this project will be £2.1 million. We have received a grant from the Heritage Lottery Fund of £970,000, and have raised a further £530,000 from other sources. Our task is to raise the £600,000 balance, and so provide the residents of Littlevillage and the surrounding area with a multi-purpose community facility which will benefit young and old for the present and in the future.

***

Chapter 3: The preparation phase

There is an old adage: time spent in reconnaissance is seldom wasted. Nowhere is this truer than in fundraising, yet you will be under pressure from the start to 'go out and raise some money'. This pressure must be resisted. Like every business operation, a fundraising campaign needs careful and detailed planning.

In Chapter Two, we covered the following key points:

- The need to ensure that your charity is in good health and ready to tackle a fundraising campaign;
- The need to define the project for which you are raising funds, and the total cost of the project;
- The people and facilities you will need to make your campaign work;
- The campaign's case for support;
- The campaign's financial programme.

All these key aspects have now been completed, and your Trustees and Campaign Management Team have agreed your Business Plan and Case Statement. Your charity is now ready for the Preparation Phase.

The Fundraising Programme

The fundraising programme is an integral part of your charity's Business Plan. Its importance is increased when you decide to embark on a fundraising campaign, as opposed to simply year-on-year fundraising activity. The fundraising programme is your campaign plan, written for all your volunteers at every level of your organisation.

No fundraising programme is likely to remain unaltered for the duration of a fundraising campaign – but that is no excuse for failing to produce a programme at the outset!

The programme is critical because:

- It concentrates the minds of your Trustees, CMT and other volunteers;
- It reminds all your volunteers of the aims of the campaign; what has to be achieved and in what timeframe; and their individual roles in this achievement. Remember – they will all be busy people and many of them will have full-time jobs. They are devoting a limited amount of quality time to your fundraising campaign and this time needs to be used to maximum effect;
- It enables your volunteers to answer questions from potential donors and grant-makers and from the media in an accurate and timely fashion and therefore add credibility to what you are trying to achieve and the progress you are making along the way.

The fundraising programme should include the following elements:
- An overall statement about how the campaign will be executed;
- The different fundraising phases and the actions in each phase;
- A timetable showing the planned start and finish not only of the campaign but of each phase within it.

You will find a fundraising programme template at the end of this chapter in Appendix A.

Research

If your campaign is to maximise its fundraising, you will need to carry out detailed research into each different source of fundraising.

Trusts and Foundations
These offer your campaign the best fundraising opportunities, for the simple reason that they exist to give grants to charities

like yours. However, while some will give grants to almost any form of charitable activity, others have quite narrow grant-making policies.

The majority of trusts and foundations - especially small ones – do not have their own websites, but do have contact telephone numbers. A call to the Correspondent is strongly advisable: not only will you be able to confirm DGMT and Charity Commission/OSCR website information, but it will also enable you to find out what specific aspects of the trust's giving areas are the trustees' current priorities. For example, do the trustees prefer revenue funding, project funding or equipment? If they support building projects, is this primarily or exclusively for purchase of buildings, refurbishment of existing buildings or construction of new buildings? You will also be able to discover dates of trustee meetings, submission deadlines and how trustees like funding applications to be framed. All this information will enable you to target each funding application most effectively.

Submissions to trusts and foundations are covered in greater depth in Chapter 5 (see p.85).

National and local government

Grants from national and local government are much reduced in the second decade of the 21st century. Both groupings tend to prefer Service Level Agreements (SLAs) whereby a charity is paid to provide specific services to the community. For many small charities, this will be inappropriate either because they are not providing services required by government or because they lack the paid staff and/or infrastructure to tender for such contracts.

Grants are still available in certain areas, and the National Council for Voluntary Organisations' (NCVO) Funding Central website gives information about grants and other contracts together with deadlines. Although grants can be substantial, the process for obtaining them is usually lengthy and complex.

Many councils at County, Unitary or District/Borough levels give their elected Councillors an annual Empowerment Fund. This allows Councillors to make grants up to a specified level for projects approved by their Council and usually – but not necessarily – in the Ward they represent. Persuading a group of councillors in one town or rural area to give a proportion of their Empowerment funding to your charity can often result in substantial sums being raised.

Submissions to national and local government are covered in greater depth in Chapter 6 (see p.101).

Individual donors

Many charity volunteers spend long hours poring over the Sunday Times Rich List, published annually in April. Sadly they are usually disappointed when the wealthy individuals thus targeted fail even to respond, let alone make a gift.

Most wealthy individuals will give to a charity with which they feel some connection. This could be a geographical link – they live, or lived, or were born in the area where your charity operates; or it could be a link to your activities - your hospice provided care for one of their dying relatives; or your charity works for children with disabilities, and they have a disabled grandchild.

Start, therefore, with a list of wealthy individuals with whom you can make a link. Then decide what you can offer them. Most wealthy philanthropists want to be assured of two things: first, the difference their gift is going to make – i.e. what will you be able to achieve with their money which you cannot without it. Secondly, how you are going to involve them in your charity in the future.

Next, find out the name(s) of their PA(s) or secretary(ies). Few if any large businesses will give out the telephone numbers of their owners or Chief Executives. Most will however give the names of the PAs or secretaries. If your first telephone call results in this information, you can confidently make your second call asking for the PA/Secretary by name. You have then the chance of selling the idea of a meeting or briefing with your target donor to the person who controls his/her diary. This is likely to be a long process which may ultimately result in little or nothing. But it has far greater chances of success than a cold-call letter.

Do not just target Rich List donors. There are many wealthy (and generous) people whose fortunes do not merit an entry in the Rich List, yet are possibly in a position to finance your entire fundraising programme several times over, if they so wished. So set up informal meetings involving Trustees, the CMT and other volunteers to explore your catchment area and the contacts they have so that you can identify potential major donors and who might best approach them on your behalf.

There will be other individual donors worth approaching, even if they are not potential major donors and are not going to give 5, 6 and 7 figure sums. You need to set up one or more evaluation groups to determine which of these individuals are worth approaching – and who is going to make the approach.

Evaluating and approaching individual donors is covered in greater depth in Chapter 8 (see p.123).

Companies

Companies are statistically the toughest fundraising nuts to crack. But they are not impossible! Start your research by finding out the companies operating in your area and who amongst your volunteers has contacts with the owners or board members

Next find out each company's charity giving track record. Do they regularly give to charities? Do they tend to give to one particular charitable area, e.g. cancer research or primary schools? Who makes the decisions on charity giving – the Board? A particular director or manager? Or do the employees vote on which charity to support? Does the company have a payroll giving scheme? Does the company manufacture or supply materials which might be of value to your project? Goods-in-kind may be a better option for both you and the company concerned, since the goods will cost the company less than the retail price you would have to pay.

Seeking corporate donations is covered in greater depth in Chapter 7 (see p.115).

Training

Running your campaign successfully means that your Trustees and volunteers will need key skills. Some of them will already have these, e.g. your Campaign Secretary should already have the necessary secretarial skills– but there are other areas where there may be a skills shortage.

- Public Relations: you will need at least one Public Relations volunteer who will be responsible for getting your campaign message across to the media, local councillors, organisations like Rotary, Lions and Round Table and other voluntary and community groups which might be persuaded to support your campaign (see p.156);
- Asking for gifts: irrespective of whether you are asking for an individual or corporate donation, the approach needs to be undertaken in the most effective way;
- Following-up gift requests;
- Organising receptions for small and large groups of potential donors;
- Organising individual fundraising events and fundraising event programmes.

Training your volunteers is covered in greater depth in Chapters 8, 10 and 11.

Planning

Having carried out the necessary research detailed above and trained your volunteers for their different tasks, the fundraising programme itself must be subject to careful and detailed planning. The critical elements of this will be:

- Agreement on the aims of the campaign and the way in which they will be realised;
- The organisation of the campaign – both in regards to volunteers and their leaders and to the campaign office from which the campaign will be run;
- The campaign strategy;
- An outline timetable, including actions to be taken and targets to be achieved in specified periods of time.

Within the campaign strategy, there needs to be an outline of the different fundraising elements and how they will fit in to the plan. For example:

- It will be wise to seek some 'leading gifts' from wealthy individuals who are actual or likely supporters. These gifts will create the important impression that the campaign is heading in a successful direction, and will encourage others to give;
- The trust fundraising campaign should concentrate initially on those trusts most likely to make a grant, and then proceed progressively towards the trusts least likely to do so;
- Community fundraising will normally begin towards the end of the campaign. The ideal situation we want to achieve is that every individual member of the campaign's constituency has either made a donation or positively declined to do so. When the community fundraising starts, those buying event tickets will have already given previously, and their contribution to fundraising events is therefore a 'second' gift.

Checklist

Fundraising Programme
- Overall statement;
- Fundraising phases and actions in each phase;
- Timetable.

Research
- Trusts and Foundations;
- National and local government;
- Individual donors;
- Companies.

Training
- Public Relations;
- Asking for gifts;
- Following up gift requests;
- Organising receptions;
- Organising events and event programmes.

Planning
- Has the implementation of the fundraising programme been effectively planned?
- Are the key elements in place?
- Are all volunteers in the campaign clear about how the fundraising programme will deliver?

Appendix A: FUNDRAISING PROGRAMME

Every fundraising campaign needs a Fundraising Programme. This follows on from the Business Plan and the Case Statement, and is the document which sets out how the fundraising campaign is to be organised and executed.

This example is based on an actual fundraising campaign.

**

BACKGROUND

Construction of All Saints' Church Littlevillage was started in the reign of King William II. Projects for rebuilding and adding to the original design took place in the 13th and 14th centuries. In 1890 the Church underwent a major restoration including the installation of a central heating system.

The Grade I listed Church boasts many fine architectural and heritage features including 14th century paintings, the 15th century nave roof and stained glass windows and an alabaster altarpiece by Charles Kempe.

Sited on a hill overlooking the village, All Saints' Church has been a centre for religious and community activities in the village for over 800 years.

CURRENT NEEDS

Despite its central location All Saints' Church has not been substantially modernised in recent years. Furthermore, the ravages of time and seasonal shifting on its shallow foundations have caused a number of structural problems.

The particular areas which require urgent attention include:
- A new roof;
- Underpinning of part of the east end of the church;
- Repointing to key areas of stonework;
- Removal and repair of stained glass windows and their frames.

The most urgent work – the new roof – needs to be undertaken within the next two years.

THE WAY AHEAD

Initial estimates indicate that the conservation and restoration work required will cost some £550,000, but it is likely that this figure may rise once surveyors and other professionals have had the chance to examine the building's problems in depth.

There is currently some £60,000 in the Church's fabric fund, and a submission to the Heritage Lottery Fund is planned.

Our future fundraising campaign will include the following key features:

Organisation

A Campaign Management Team (CMT) will be formed to determine the direction and policy of the Campaign. The CMT will report to the Parochial Church Council (PCC), and will consist of some 7 members: Chairman; Campaign treasurer; PR representative; Major Gifts representative; Research leader; Community fundraising representative; Campaign Secretary.

At least two Taskforces will be recruited. The first (Major Gifts) will target businesses and wealthy individuals in Littlevillage and the surrounding area; whilst the second (Community) will take charge of community fundraising including an events programme.

We intend to appoint a Patron and Vice Patrons from amongst the 'great & good' of Littlevillage and the surrounding area. Possible candidates for Patron might include the Lord Lieutenant for Bigcounty or a celebrity with a Littlevillage connection.

A fully-equipped Campaign Office will be set up in the Church Hall, which will serve as the focal point for those involved in the Campaign, either as volunteers or donors. The Campaign Secretary will run the Campaign Office and ensure continuity and effective administrative back-up for the Campaign.

Strategy

Successful fundraising is based on targeting all possible sources of funding for the Campaign, and pursuing these methodically until all potential donors have either given or positively declined to give. Set out below are the groups we intend to target for our campaign

- *Individual donors.* There are a number of wealthy individuals living in Bigcounty, some of whom have specific connections with Littlevillage;

- *Corporate donors.* A number of international size companies are based in Bigcounty. There are smaller national and local businesses in the industrial estates to the north and east of the village;

- *Grant-making trusts.* Apart from UK-wide trusts which make grants to a broad spectrum of charitable activities, there are a number of trusts which specifically make grants to projects in Bigcounty; to heritage projects; and to projects linked to the Church of England and places of worship;

- *Statutory Fundraising.* Grants are available not only from Government and European sources, but also from local government at county, district/borough and town/parish levels;

- *The National Lottery.* Although grants from the National Lottery have been much reduced in recent years, there are still opportunities for funding through the Big Lottery, the Heritage Lottery Fund and the *Awards for All* programme;

- *Community Campaign.* All Saints' Church once restored will offer the people of Littlevillage much more than a centre of worship, important though that is. The size of the Church lends itself to public performances and community events from which everyone of all different faiths or no religious beliefs at all can benefit.

OUTLINE TIMETABLE

A detailed timetable will be produced once the fundraising programme has been agreed. However, our intended timeframe to achieve our fundraising target is as follows:

Months 1-3:
- Plan Campaign strategy;
- Set up Campaign organisation and Campaign Office;
- Appoint Campaign Secretary;
- Research funding sources;
- Evaluate individual and corporate donors;
- Evaluate and recruit Fundraising Taskforce;
- Recruit Patron and Vice Patrons;
- Produce Campaign literature;
- Congregation make individual donations;
- Initial approaches to grant-making trusts;
- Public Launch of Campaign.

Months 4-6:
- Fundraising Taskforce approaches to individual and corporate donors;
- Further approaches to grant-making trusts;
- Evaluate and recruit Community Taskforce;
- Seek funds from local government and other sources.

Months 6-12:
- Community Taskforce initiates community fundraising;
- Continue grant-making trust approaches.

Chapter 4: First steps

A key ingredient in successful fundraising is the ability to sell your cause and your project. But there is a vital difference between your sales pitch and business selling.

In business, you are trying to persuade people to part with their money, for which they receive either goods or services in return.

In charity fundraising, they part with their money but receive only the warm glow of having supported a worthwhile cause.

So your cause or project has to have a watertight case. You have already produced and agreed your Case Statement but there are still some other steps you need to take before you start asking others for support.

Previous fundraising

This may be your charity's first fundraising campaign but it is unlikely that it will never have raised any funds previously.

Start therefore by checking on previous fundraising records and ensuring that all previous donors have been thanked and, where appropriate, recognised. Many trusts and corporate and public funders include recognition such as wall plaques as a grant condition. Your campaign will not get off to a good start if previous donors feel that their generosity has not been appreciated and are therefore disinclined to support your new venture.

Good housekeeping

Many potential donors – individual, corporate and trust – will want to see your charity's annual report and accounts and will scrutinise these closely. Wealthy philanthropists are wealthy because they are careful where they put their money, and donors will wish to assure themselves that your charity is a tight financial ship.

Start then by checking when your services were last put out to tender or compared with their competitors. These could include:

- Electricity;
- Gas;
- Water;
- Telephone and broadband;
- Internal cleaning;
- Buildings maintenance;
- External grounds maintenance;
- Supply of consumables, especially items such as printer ink and toner, paper, cleaning materials.

In this way you will minimise your charity's revenue expenditure, with the result that more of your income will be available for your fundraising project.

Existing income

Before you start approaching new potential donors or asking existing donors to give more, ensure that the effectiveness of existing donors' current gifts is maximised. This will include:

- Making sure that you claim Gift Aid on all gifts from donors who are UK taxpayers. Checks on previous donations where allowable Gift Aid has not been claimed can often result in a valuable 'windfall';
- Suggesting to donors who are 40% or 50% rate taxpayers that they give the relief they receive (i.e. the difference between the basic rate and what they are paying) to your charity instead of hanging on to it;

- Ensuring that casual donors (e.g. if you are a church that has occasional Sunday churchgoers from outside your parish) complete Gift Aid forms/envelopes so that you can claim their tax too;
- Claiming Gift Aid on unnamed small gifts in collection boxes and tins (the Gift Aid Small Donations Scheme) (see p.144t);
- Checking your bank accounts to ensure that the minimum necessary funds are deposited in your current account, whilst the maximum are either invested or are deposited in high interest bearing savings accounts.

Tax efficient giving schemes

In addition to collecting Gift Aid, you will need to be able to give potential donors information about tax efficient methods of giving or, at the very least, signpost them to where they might find out (see p.143).

Many individuals and companies will not wish to give cash directly, and there are a number of ways in which both categories of donor can give using alternative methods:

- Individuals can make gifts of publicly quoted shares, which your charity can then sell. This is a very tax-efficient method of giving, since the shares will not only be exempt from capital gains tax liability, but will also qualify the donor for tax relief on their value at the time of gifting;
- Individuals can also transfer assets such as property and works of art without incurring capital gains tax. Outright gifts, including bequests, are exempt from inheritance tax (IHT);
- Companies can claim corporation tax relief on gifts to charity;
- Companies can also set up payroll giving schemes. These are relatively easy to organise and do not incur a heavy workload for a company's finance department as the administrative burden falls on an approved Payroll Giving Agency

(PGA). Employees' regular giving is deducted at source and payroll giving schemes offer charities a regular monthly income over a long period of time, except in those industries where staff turnover is high, e.g. hospitality or hairdressing;

• Companies may also prefer to give in-kind. This can be advantageous both to the company and the charity, e.g. bricks make up around 80% of the cost of a new build, so bricks donated or sold at cost could reduce a campaign target considerably;

• If your project involves building, conservation or restoration work, your CMT needs to be aware of the VAT rules which apply to these different activities.

Brief details on Gift Aid, VAT and Payroll Giving are at Appendix A to this chapter. Tax efficient giving and VAT rules are covered in greater depth in Chapter 9 (see p.143).

Use of facilities

Do you have a building or open space, all or part of which could be used by your charity or by others to generate income? It will impress potential donors to your fundraising campaign if you are able to demonstrate that your facilities are already working to create an income. For example:

• A school I know well has an assembly and activities hall which they let out in the evenings and at week-ends to a wide variety of after-school clubs and local community and sports groups. This produces a healthy income which exceeds their heating, lighting and janitorial costs. A few years ago they received Local Education Authority funds to build two new classrooms. The Governors and Head decided on a specification which included lavatories, a small kitchen area and an outside entrance which could be accessed even when the rest of the school was closed. The two classrooms could easily be converted into a wide variety of community and voluntary uses. They proved to be extremely popular owing to the lack of similar, cost-effective facilities elsewhere in the town – and also because of the tea, coffee and snack-making opportunities in the kitchen area. As a result, even more income was generated for the school;

• At the church where I attend Sunday service, enthusiastic members of the congregation decided some years ago to plant unused parts of the churchyard with snowdrops. These proliferated and a number are now dug up annually and sold over a February week-end. Cream teas are provided for visitors and potential purchasers. This event regularly produced £350 surplus on the basis of sales of snowdrops and teas on one Saturday. It was then decided to extend the event to a whole week-end, and the event was publicised via a local radio station. As a result of these two decisions, the surplus generated increased to £4,000;

• A homeless charity decided to involve the people it helped in income generating activities which would financially benefit the individual homeless people as well as the charity's overall work for the homeless. These activities included outside catering and the repair, refurbishment and resale of garden tools donated by the public. The activities provided a regular revenue stream which it is difficult to achieve through more conventional fundraising means such as major gifts campaigns and trust/foundation funding applications.

Recycling

Government legislation over recent years has led to increased recycling by local authorities. However, there are numerous opportunities for charities to derive income from recycling schemes which cost them nothing.

• *Printer ink and toner cartridges.* There are on-line organisations which will provide collection containers and a collection service free-of-charge to charities. Payments are then made to charities on the basis of the number and type of cartridges collected;

- *Mobile phones.* These are slightly more valuable than ink and toner cartridges. You can check on-line the value of any particular mobile. Usually recycling companies will give more money for a mobile in its box with its charger and other ancillaries than it will for the mobile on its own;
- *Clothing.* In the mid-20th century clothes in almost any condition could be sold for re-use. However, the advent of very cheap clothing available from some chain stores means that only clothing which is in very good condition and, preferably, with a designer label can be re-sold. The exception to this is babies' and young children's clothing, for which there is always a ready market. There are also clothing recycling companies which will take old clothing and other textiles including boots and shoes, and pay charities for these on the basis of the weight of textiles involved;
- *Cars.* In 2009, the Giveacar scheme was launched. Owners of serviceable scrap cars can give the proceeds to charities when Giveacar sells them on their behalf.

Recycling is covered in greater depth in Chapter 11 (see p.178).

And finally … remember than one of the secrets of successful fundraising is 'concurrent activity'. This means that for maximum effectiveness you should where possible run a number of different activities in parallel rather than in sequence. For example:

- While your Trustees are undertaking their good housekeeping checks, your Treasurer should be reviewing the effectiveness of concurrent gifts and how this could be improved;
- As you are reviewing existing and potential future use of your charity's facilities, some volunteers are researching potential grants from trusts and foundations, and others are researching possible corporate donors in your area.

As your timetable shows, there are certain activities which can only be undertaken successfully once another activity or sequence of activities is complete. However, there are many aspects to your campaign which can take place in parallel – and your CMT and Campaign Office will need to plan to ensure that this happens.

Checklist

Good Housekeeping
- Utilities checked for value or put out to tender;
- Cleaning and maintenance contracts reviewed/re-tendered;
- Contracts with suppliers of consumables reviewed.

Existing income
- Gift Aid claimed on all gifts from UK taxpayers;
- Extra relief requested from 40% and 50% taxpayers;
- Gift Aid claimed on gifts from casual donors;
- Gift Aid claimed on small, unnamed gifts;
- Bank accounts checked for best rates of interest.

Tax efficient giving schemes
- CMT and Campaign Office briefed on alternative gift options for individuals;
- Corporate donors aware of corporation tax relief;
- Corporate donors briefed on payroll giving schemes;
- CMT consider gifts in-kind;
- CMT fully aware of VAT regulations for charities on construction, conservation or restoration work.

Use of facilities
- Buildings and/or land let out for rent;
- Land used for fundraising;
- Other fundraising activities involving volunteers or beneficiaries.

Recycling

- Existing recycling fundraising checked for best returns;
- Printer ink and toner cartridges;
- Mobile 'phones;
- Clothing/textiles;
- Cars.

Appendix A: HMRC and PAYROLL GIVING

Gift Aid

The HMRC website gives detailed information about Gift Aid in general. It also covers specifically:
*   The Gift Aid Small Donations Scheme;
*   The Gift Aid on-line scheme which results in quicker repayment of Gift Aid to charities.

Go to the HMRC home page and then select 'Charities and donors' from the Quick Links option box. Then from the menu select the relevant items relating to Gift Aid.

VAT

The HMRC website gives guidance for charities on VAT. To access this, go to HMRC home page and then select 'Charities and donors' from the Quick Links option box. Then from the menu select 'VAT guidance for charities and not-for-profit organisations'. The following areas are covered:
*   VAT for charities and not-for-profit organisations: introduction. What VAT reliefs and exemptions are available on expenditure or income, whether you should register for VAT;
*   VAT treatment of common types of charity income. What income for charities and not-for-profit organisations is taxable, exempt or outside the scope of VAT;
*   How VAT applies to fundraising events. How charities and not-for-profit organisations can be exempt from charging VAT on fundraising events that meet certain conditions;
*   VAT reliefs on charity purchases. What goods and services are VAT zero-rated or reduced-rated when purchased by charities;
*   Zero-rated VAT on charity-funded equipment. What goods and services qualify for zero-rating if bought with charitable funds by or for certain types of organization;

- Reduced rate VAT on fuel and power used for charity non-business use. Who qualifies for reduced rate VAT, working out the split between business and non-business use, what types of supply qualify;
- How charities can import goods VAT-free. What types of goods can be bought VAT-free and who can import them;
- Charging VAT if you make supplies to charities. Supplying goods to charities at a reduced or zero rate of VAT, checking that the charity and your supplies qualify for relief.

Payroll Giving

Payroll giving offers an effective way for a charity to raise a regular monthly income through established businesses.

The majority of business with more than 500 employees have payroll giving schemes. However, the majority of small/medium size businesses (SMEs) do not. The scheme is good for charities because:

- Monthly donations are deducted before tax, so there is no Gift Aid for charities to claim and gifts are worth more to the charity than they cost the donors;
- Once a scheme is in place, it usually runs uninterrupted for many years. The exception to this is in high turnover industries such as the hospitality industry and hairdressing;
- Statistics show that employees rarely cancel payroll giving.

The scheme is good for companies because:

- A Payroll Giving Agency (PGA) is selected from an approved list. The PGA processes all the paperwork; provides support to charities and employers in setting up the scheme; and provides disbursement statements to charities so that donors and payments can be tracked;
- The company chooses the PGA and signs a contract with them;
- The company simply has to send the donated money to the PGA within 14 days of the end of the income tax month;

- The company is seen to have a positive policy towards charity giving.

Chapter 5: Trusts and foundations

Trusts and foundations (known collectively as grant-making trusts or GMTs) are a good start for your fundraising campaign because they themselves are registered charities whose sole purpose is to give grants to charities like yours.

There are over 2,500 trusts and foundations in the UK and this figure increases by around 50 per year. Collectively they give out around £3 billion annually. You should achieve a 1:4 hit-rate if you carry out your research in sufficient depth.

However, there is a downside:
•   Demand for grants far outstrips the funds available from GMTs;
•   Grant funds are mainly derived from the annual income from investments. So in a recession when the demand for grants is greatest, GMTs' income is usually at a low ebb;
•   You are trying to convince a Board of Trustees, none of whom you are likely to have met, that they should give money to your charity in preference to other worthy causes;
•   You don't know which other charities are applying for funds at the same time as you and therefore you have no inkling as to the size or scope of the competition.

All this means that you must carry out detailed research on GMTs likely to support your charity, and you must develop the ability to get your key messages across concisely, succinctly and convincingly in a short application form or in a letter of two sides of A4 or less.

In addition to trusts and foundations, there are the City of London Livery Companies, which are wealthy and generous donors. Some of these have their own charitable trusts.

Whilst some Livery Companies support projects only in the City of London or in Greater London, a substantial number give to projects all over the UK and overseas. Many will consider small, local charities, particularly if your project has tangible community benefits.

Information on City Livery Companies can be gained as follows:

• The City of London has produced a booklet 'City Livery Companies' which is available free by calling the City of London Public Relations Office on 0207 606 3030;

• The Worshipful Company of Fishmongers (www.fishhall.org.uk) has a link on its website which provides a list of all the Livery Companies, together with links to their contact details and websites, where applicable. At the bottom of the Fishmongers' website Home Page, click on 'Sitemap' and then approximately three quarters of the way down the left hand column click on 'Livery Companies' Database'. Some Livery Companies accept funding applications by letter or e-mail, while others have gone over to an on-line only system.

Research tools

Books

There are a number of books which will assist in your research. The principal of these, published by the Directory of Social Change (DSC), are:

• The Directory of Grant Making Trusts (DGMT). This is the so-called 'bible' of trust fundraising, and should be sufficient for the needs of most small charities. DGMT is published every two years and a new copy costs around £125.00. However, used copies of earlier editions around 4-5 years old can be bought second-hand through Amazon and other sources for around £12.00: these should be perfectly sufficient for a one-off fundraising campaign;

- Guide to the Major Trusts Volumes 1 & 2. This guide is in a larger format and is divided into two volumes: Volume 1 lists the 400 largest trusts in the UK, which individually give out £300,000 or more per year. Volume 2 lists a further 1100 trusts. The combined new cost of the Guide is £125.00, with each separate volume costing £75.00.

Websites

There are essentially two types of websites available for your campaign. These are:

- Free websites. The Charity Commission for England and Wales and the Office of the Scottish Charity Regulator both run free access websites. These give a wide range of information about charities (including GMTs) in the respective countries. The Charity Commission website also offers contact details, lists of trustees and access to annual accounts. However, these websites need to be used in conjunction with the books referred to above, as they do not provide any search mechanism to identify which trusts are likely to make a grant to your fundraising campaign. Funding Central – funded by the Office of the Third Sector – covers national and local funding and finance opportunities for charities and voluntary organisations from charitable, local government, regional, national and European sources. You can also sign up to receive a weekly newsletter and funding alerts which match funding criteria in which your charity is interested and which you have inputted;
- Subscription websites. These are research websites and will provide you with a range of funding information. Examples of such websites include:

www.trustfunding.org.uk
www.governmentfunding.org.uk
www.companygiving.org.uk

Trust application plan

As previously mentioned, there are over 2,500 GMTs in the UK. Some will not give to your charity either because your activities do not match their grant-giving criteria or because they do not make grants in your geographical area. Nonetheless, this will leave you with a large number of potential grant-makers.

Your plan can be created and its implementation begun whilst research on GMTs is still taking place. You should have a list of priorities, with the top priority being GMTs most likely to support your cause. Your plan should look like this:

1. GMTs which have given to your charity in the past. Even if you have never run a fundraising campaign, there is always the likelihood that someone in the past has applied for grants. Contrary to some popularly held views, GMTs which have given to your charity in the past are more – not less - likely to give to you again. Check to see whether the GMT insists on a specific time lapse between your previous grant and your application for the next one.

2. GMTs which give to charities in your county. This should be an early priority because you have already met one criterion in that your charity is located in the county they favour.

3. GMTs which give to charities in your region /country Here you are casting your net wider, but still fulfilling a vital criterion. There will be more competition in a region than a county – but less than UK-wide. If your charity is raising funds for an overseas project, start with GMTs which give to projects in the country where you are working or supporting work.

4. GMTs which give to charities working in your field or to charities whose beneficiaries are the same as yours. These are the GMTs which will be closest to what you do and those you are trying to help. DGMT lists the categories, which need to be examined thoroughly for maximum benefit. For example, if you are a primary school raising funds for a sports

hall, you will want to approach GMTs which give grants to Primary and Secondary Education. But you should also contact GMTs which give grants to Sports Education; Recreation and Sport; Recreational facilities; Sports. If your school is a faith school; you intend to offer the use of the hall to the community for sporting and other activities; some of your pupils or community groups wanting to use the hall have disabilities; or you intend to stage regular intergenerational activities, then the following categories may be applicable too: Faith schools; Christianity (or another faith if applicable); Ecumenicalism; Community and social centres; Sport for people with a disability; Services for and about children and young people; activities and relationships between generations. The beneficiaries might include: Children; Young people; Sportsmen and Women; People who are disabled; Parents; People living in rural (urban) areas; People who are unemployed.

5.   GMTs which give to General Charitable Projects (GCPs). These trusts represent the majority and will, with some specific exceptions, give to any charity they consider deserving and with a project worth supporting. The Garfield Weston Foundation, one of the wealthiest in the world, is a case in point: they will in principle consider a grant to any charity except animal welfare charities and charities working outside the UK.

You will note that in DGMT, each category beyond geographical variations has 2 sections: the GMTs for which that category is a funding priority; and those which will consider that particular type of activity our beneficiary. Your list therefore should include 2 approach phases: the first for the 'priority' GMTs and the second for the 'consider' ones.

Further research

So, you have researched your lists of trusts in DGMT. What next? One of DGMT's limitations is that it relies for its accuracy on the trusts it lists responding to its annual request for updated information. Some of these trusts seldom if ever respond, so DGMT simply reprints the information from the previous edition.

You need to confirm DGMT's information, and you achieve this through checking the entry of each GMT you intend contacting on the Charity Commission or OSCR website. This will not only enable you to check each GMT's contact details, but you will also be able to highlight any anomalies in the GMT's DGMT entry as compared with the details on the relevant website.

Finally, you telephone each GMT. This is vital. Try and speak to the GMT's Correspondent or Administrator, rather than an intern, to establish whether it would be worthwhile your charity submitting a funding application and, if so, a number of key points such as what particular aspects of your fundraising campaign are likely to interest their trustees and how they like a submission put together. Ensure that you make a note of the date and time of your call and the person you spoke to – you will need this in the submission.

Before you make your call, look at the GMT's own website if it has one. If it does, the correspondent will simply tell you to look at it. If you can say at the beginning: 'I've looked at your website and there are just one or two points where I would be glad of clarification …..', you have got off on the right foot.

There are some GMTs which do not provide either a telephone contact number or an e-mail address either in DGMT or the Charity Commission and OSCR websites. In these cases, a speculative letter is the only option – although these tend to produce less positive results than letters following an initial telephone call.

An *aide mémoire* on trust research and a trust telephone script and record sheet are at the end of this chapter in Appendix A.

Making your submission

Before putting pen to paper (or hand to keyboard), make sure that you have:
- Checked the notes you made in your telephone conversation with each GMT's representative;
- Check with their written guidelines (if they publish any) about how the GMT likes the submission made. If, for example, it says that hardcopy submissions are accepted but e-mailed ones preferred, choose the latter: there is no point in doing something which the funder finds less attractive and thus disadvantages your charity in comparison with other applicants;
- Send the GMT only what is requested. If the guidelines ask for two sides of A4 and a copy of your most recent annual accounts, do not on the one hand forget the accounts, or on the other send additional literature, DVDs or lengthy letters which they have not requested.

Your application

Most GMTs request a short letter (i.e. two sides of A4) or completion of an application form. Here are some guidelines for these two types of application:

Letter
You need to get the following across:
- Your charity name and what it does;
- A brief description of your project;
- Why the project is necessary;
- What is it going to cost;
- Who are the beneficiaries;

- Whether you are asking the GMT to make a grant to the project as a whole, or to some specific aspect of it.

Don't forget to start by referring to the telephone conversation you had with the GMT's representative during your research phase.

It is also important to re-write appropriate parts of your trust letter to reflect a particular GMT's interests or points raised in your telephone conversation. Most GMT trustees will spot a standard mail-merged letter a mile off!

On the whole, it is best if the head of your charity (Chairman, Chief Executive, Headmaster/Headmistress, Vicar, Minister, Rabbi, Imam) signs the letter and 'tops and tails' it in manuscript.

A sample trust letter is at the end of this chapter in Appendix B.

Application form

- Do answer the questions they ask – not what you have pre-prepared!
- Do keep to the number of words specified in each section, where appropriate;
- If the form cannot be completed on-line, find a volunteer with very neat handwriting;
- Write a short covering letter to go with the form, again referring to the telephone conversation in your research phase;
- Ensure the form as well as the letter is signed (if appropriate) and check that additional paperwork requested has been included;
- Some GMTs have on-line forms which cannot be downloaded. These can, however, be saved so that they do not need to be completed at one sitting. You will need to enter your e-mail address and a password; most also require up-loading of supporting documents such as annual accounts, so it is wise to have these available on your computer.

Checklist

Research tools
- Acquired copy of DGMT;
- Considered subscription websites;
- Set up funding e-mail alerts.

Application plan
- List of GMTs which have made past grants;
- List of GMTs funding charities in your county;
- List of GMTs funding charities in your region or country (overseas);
- List of GMTs funding charities working in your field/with your beneficiaries;
- Separate lists of *Funding Priority* and *Will Consider*.

Further research
- Checked DGMT details on Charity Commission/OSCR;
- Looked at GMTs' websites where applicable;
- Telephoned GMTs;
- Completed telephone record sheets.

Application letters
- Checked guidelines for applications;
- Amended generic letter to reflect telephone conversation/website information;
- Agreed with Chairman or other leader date/time for signing letters;
- Enclosed other documents requested by GMT.

Application forms
- Completed on-line or hard copy;
- Section word numbers not exceeded;
- Form signed if in hard copy;
- Produced covering letter;
- If on-line submission, additional documents up-loaded.

Appendix A: RESEARCHING GRANT-MAKING TRUSTS

The *Aide Mémoire* and telephone script below have been created to assist volunteers in researching trusts and foundations. The precise details should be amended to fit in with your specific fundraising campaign.

***

ALL SAINTS' CHURCH, LITTLEVILLAGE

Campaign Office Research

1.   The principal tool for Trust research is The Directory of Grant-Making Trusts (DGMT), copies of which are in the Campaign Office and the Public Library.

2.   DGMT is broken down into different sections.

3.   The main section gives full details of Trusts in alphabetical order, including their contact details and registered charity number.

4.   Subsidiary sections list all trusts geographically and also by the type of charitable activity to which they make grants.

5.   We need initially to research trusts geographically, i.e. the ones which make grants to charitable projects in Bigcounty specifically or anywhere in our region.

6.   After this, we will need to research under the categories which fit into our project. These will be heritage and the built environment (especially religious buildings); religious education; faith activities; social welfare (some categories); community centres and activities; beneficial groups (especially children, young people, older people); faith; social or economic circumstances.

7.   Copy the Trusts falling into appropriate categories onto a piece of paper, noting their charity number alongside from the main section of DGMT.

Home research

This research follows on from the Campaign Office research and can be undertaken from home.

1.   Using your computer, access the Charity Commission website on the internet, tap in the registered charity number of each trust in turn.

2.   On the first page, details are given of any restrictions on grant giving. For example, a trust giving grants to an ecclesiastical project might only consider outreach and not building projects. Clearly we do not wish to contact those trusts which make it clear that a project like ours is not for them.

3.   If the trust has no restrictions which would preclude them giving us a grant, go to the contact page for the trust, using the click box on the left hand side of the first page.

4.   Download the contact page (this can be done on rough or scrap paper).

Telephoning Trusts

1.   Armed with the contact page for each Trust from the Charity Commission website, telephone each trust in turn.

2.   When the Trust answers, please ensure you complete the telephone pro-forma fully and accurately. This is most important because the detailed results of your telephone conversation will form the basis of our Trust applications.

3.   A copy of the telephone proforma is attached.

4.   Telephone calls may be undertaken from your own home, or from the Campaign Office by arrangement with the Campaign Secretary.

5.   If you are connected to an answering machine, please leave a message asking the person either to call you, or the Campaign Office, back. If you are asking them to call the Campaign Office, please let the Campaign Secretary know that he/she should expect a call from a particular trust and, possibly, a specific person.

6.   Try and engage the people you are speaking to in a friendly conversation and tease out of them what aspects of our

project their trustees might find particularly attractive. However, there is no point in engaging in a long conversation if the person you are speaking to makes it clear that the trustees have no grant funds left, or would not support our type of project, or both. If the person at the trust indicates that a submission now would fail, but a future one might be successful, try and find out the timeframe in which we should be applying.

ALL SAINTS' CHURCH, LITTLEVILLAGE

TRUST/FOUNDATION GRANT APPLICATIONS

Telephone Script

Caller: ....

Date of call: ....

Trust/Foundation: ....

Telephone no: ....

Person you spoke to: ....

Hello, my name is .... and I am calling from All Saints' Church in Littlevillage, Bigcounty. Our Church is early Norman in origin, although it was rebuilt in 1250 and extended between 1300 and 1390. It contains rare 14th century paintings, stained glass and an alabaster altarpiece by Charles Kempe, as well as other fine features. We need to raise £550,000 for a new roof; to underpin the east end of the Church and repair the stained glass windows and frames so that its use can be extended for religious and community purposes.

Are we the sort of charity your Trustees might consider supporting?

[*REPLY: No*]

Thank you for your advice. Can you tell me what sort of charities your Trustees do support?

....

....

[*REPLY Yes*]

Great. Can you please advise me:

1.   The name of the person I should write to (*double check spelling name, title, address*)

....

....

2.   The deadline for submission for the next Trustees' meeting:

....

3. How do Trustees prefer applications to be submitted?
*   Letter: [*If yes, how long?*]
*   Application form
*   On-line

4. What additional documentation would the Trustees like?

....

....

5. Are there any particular aspect(s) of our work we should emphasise?

....

....

6. Do you advise we ask for a specific amount or just a general request?

....

....

General comments on your telephone conversation:

....

....

....

Appendix B: SAMPLE TRUST LETTER

(date)

The Correspondent
XYZ Charitable Trust
1 Any Street
Any Town
Anyshire AA1 1AA

Dear (in mss)

I am writing following a telephone conversation on 1 August 2013 between Alice Smith and my colleague Victoria Harding to ask if the Trustees of the XYZ Charitable Trust would consider making a grant to Littlevillage Guildhall Trust.

Littlevillage Guildhall Trust (registered charity no 1234560) has its charitable origins in the 15th Century, although the Trust was not established as a registered charity until 1956. The charity is responsible for the maintenance of the 15th Century Grade 1 listed Littlevillage Guildhall.

The Guildhall has been the centre of village life in Littlevillage for over 500 years. It is one of very few 15th century timber-framed Guildhalls in the United Kingdom still largely in its original state. It is the one of the oldest secular buildings in Bigcounty, and a major visitor attraction in the area, drawing hundreds of tourist annually from the rest of the UK and overseas.

An earlier restoration project in the mid-20th Century saved the building from collapse. Unfortunately, the work carried out had some long-term side effects, owing to the modern materials which were used but which were subsequently showed to be incompatible with the original 15th century construction techniques and materials.

Once complete, the conserved Guildhall will provide Littlevillage and the surrounding villages with a Library and Museum on the ground floor together with a venue on the first floor for meetings, exhibitions, arts performances and functions. We will also include insulation and heating systems which are environmentally appropriate to a Grade 1 listed building, together with a kitchen, WCs, new staircase and pneumatic lift to give total access to the building for people with disabilities, wheelchair users and parents with small children, prams and buggies.

The total cost of our project is £2.1 million. Towards this figure we have received a grant from the Heritage Lottery Fund of £970,000, and our fundraising efforts to date have raised a further £530,000. However, this means that we still have some £600,000 to raise and we believe that we are unlikely to achieve this figure in the timeframe set by the Heritage Lottery Fund without outside help.

I very much hope that your Trustees will consider our case sympathetically. Littlevillage Guildhall is a unique building, both historically and architecturally, which we are determined to preserve for present and future use, not only for residents of Littlevillage but for the wider public who visit our village.

With best wishes,

Yours sincerely, (in mss)

GAVIN LESTER
Chairman of Trustees

Chapter 6: Statutory funds, the National Lottery and funds from Europe

Statutory sources, the National Lottery and the European Union all run grant programmes from which your charity can benefit. Substantial grants are available, in many cases much larger than the grants you could expect to receive from most GMTs. However, there are downsides:

- Much of the funding from these three organisations comes in very specific, time-limited programmes. So if your project doesn't match the precise aims of the funding programmes, or you need funds in a different timeframe from the programme schedule, you miss out;
- Some funding programmes are announced with very short submission times, e.g. six weeks. So if you do not find out about these until well into the submission period, you could be burning the midnight oil to meet the deadline;
- The money disbursed by these sources is, in the last analysis, taxpayers' money. So government and local government departments, Lottery funds and the European Union have to exercise care when making grants. Whilst this care is right and proper, it means that application forms and processes are usually long and complex, and decision-making times lengthy. If therefore you need to raise funds within a specific – and fairly short – timeframe, these sources of funding may be not for you.

However, there are exceptions, so read on.

Statutory sources

Statutory funding falls into two main categories:

National Government
These are funds provided by different ministries and departments, often in response to the Government's desire to promote some particular activity and/or policy. Few are continuous, and most tend to come and go as governments, ministers and political objectives change. An increasing number are linked to the provision of services by charities, frequently services previously provided by the public sector.

Local government.
Most of the UK has a three tier local government system: county councils; district/borough councils; and town/parish councils. However, there are an increasing number of Unitary Authorities where a single council fulfils the roles of all 3 tiers. Examples of this include Luton and Milton Keynes. Local authorities tend to have fewer outright grant programmes and more Service Level Agreements (SLAs) where the authority, often in partnership with other statutory bodies in their area, e.g. the NHS, will pay charities to provide services for local people. Such services include advice centres, community transport and personal and domestic care for people in their homes. A number of local authorities have created so-called 'empowerment funds'. These are funds which are given to each councillor annually for him/her to give to projects in their Ward or neighbouring area which will benefit their constituents. These are outright grants and are given at councillors' discretion, although the receiving projects must be approved by the council concerned. Empowerment funds can be quite generous, with sums of up to £10,000 per councillor being available.

National Government Statutory funds application plan

Most of the major government departments and ministries have statutory grant programmes – but some of these will be inappropriate for your charity. Your plan should look like this:

- Access appropriate funding websites, e.g. www.governmentfunding.org.uk (subscription)
www.gov.uk/browse/citizenship/government/government-funding-programmes (free)
www.fundingcentral.org.uk (free)
- Websites like these have details of all the government departments and their responsibilities, thus enabling you to concentrate on those departments whose responsibilities cover your charity's area. For example, if your charity provides services for homeless people, it is possible that the Department for Communities and Local Government; the Department of Education; and the Department of Health might all have programmes which could fund all or some of your activities. Equally, it is unlikely that the Foreign & Commonwealth Office will do so;
- So start by checking out those departments likely to have a grant programme which might fit with your charity. This will allow you to eliminate Departments and funding streams outside your charity's sphere;
- Make a shortlist of grants for which your charity is eligible, which meet your needs and where the application and decision-making timeframes match your timelines;
- Then call the Department or programme numbers to establish your charity's eligibility, and discover any key points about making your application which are not covered on websites;
- Finally – submit your application.

Local Government statutory funds application plan

Unless you live in a Unitary Authority, you will have the possibility of accessing statutory funding at three levels: county; district (rural) or borough (urban); and town (urban) or parish (rural).

These three tiers will not have identical grant programmes, nor will they necessarily have the same charitable or local priorities. So each level has to be approached separately and treated like a different funder as you would do with GMTs.

Council grant programmes have reduced in recent years, while SLAs have increased. This means that your charity's chances of major local government funding are substantially less than they were, say, 10 years ago – unless it is actually delivering a service the local authority wants.

Councils are very sensitive about inclusivity – and this means that you will need to explain how your charity's project benefits the whole community and not just those most obviously associated with it; and how disabled and disadvantaged groups in particular will be able to access and benefit from your project. This is particularly important for schools, churches and other places of worship, and sports clubs.

Your plan should look like this:

• Taking each council in your area at a time, find out from its website what grants it offers;

• Have a look at its Strategic Plan and see where your charity might be able to assist with some of its objectives. This might be general – the council is trying to increase people's participation in sport and you are a sports club – or specific: you are wanting funds to refurbish your church hall and the Council is looking for a venue in your town or village where they can set up computer lessons for the over 65s;

• Find out the name and contact details of the council officer responsible for the relevant programmes/grants you have researched, and then make an appointment to go and see him/her. This is most important: you will gain a much greater insight about the Council's aims and the funding possibilities that go with them from a face-to-face meeting than you will ever do by letter, e-mail or telephone. Furthermore, you will learn about 'council-speak' and how they view their grant funding. For example, some years ago I was seeking a council grant for a local charity. We had to meet a minimum of four criteria of a possible ten set down. I didn't see that we met more than two – but when I met the relevant council officer, she offered an entirely different perspective on each criterion, showing me than if viewed from the Council's standpoint, we actually met nine out of ten criteria. We later received a grant!

• When you reach the Town/Parish tier of local government, you will probably find that there is little or nothing in the way of grant programmes. It is more likely that the council will simply allocate a sum from its annual budget for local charities. Furthermore, the Mayor or Chairman will probably select one or more local charities for his/her term of office for which he/she will run fundraising events during the year. You need to approach the Town Clerk or Clerk to the Parish Council and find out at which meeting in the year the Council decides on its charitable giving – and then ensure you submit a good case, having briefed your Ward councillor beforehand so that he/she can speak on your behalf. You also need to find out the name of the next Mayor or Chairman (usually, but not always, the current Deputy) so that you can approach him/her before they take office and encourage them to have your charity as their charity, or one of their charities, of the year.

If one or more of the councils in your area has an empowerment fund for councillors, this is also an excellent source of financial support. Key points are:

• Approach those councillors in whose Ward your charity is located and additionally those councillors whose constituents do or could benefit from your charity's work in general and fundraising project in particular;

• Do not approach councillors for a project for which their council is already providing you with a grant;

• Approach in February/March when councillors may have part of their empowerment fund for the current financial year unspent with the prospect of having to hand it back at the end of the year; and also after the beginning of the financial year before other charities get in first! The effect of a councillor's donation and any publicity you give it during an election year is also worth remembering.

Empowerment funds are a relatively new idea, and many councils have not yet embraced them. The funds are a potentially valuable source of funding if your council operates them.

The Landfill Communities Fund

Formerly known at the Landfill Tax Credit Scheme (LTCS), the Landfill Communities Fund (LCF) was set up in 1996, following the introduction of tax on landfill waste as a means to reduce the amount of land-filled waste and to promote a shift to more environmentally sustainable methods of waste management.

The fund is a tax credit scheme which enables operators of landfill sites to contribute money to enrolled Environmental Bodies (EBs) to carry out projects that meet environmental objects contained in the Landfill Tax Regulations.

Any charity can apply to the regulatory body Entrust to be an EB. However, this is usually unnecessary as Landfill Operators (LOs) take out a membership to cover all charities likely to apply to them.

The Government saw the LCF as a way for LOs and EBs to work in partnership to create significant environmental benefits and jobs and to undertake projects which improve the lives of communities living near landfill sites.

LOs can contribute up to 6.8% of their landfill tax liability to EBs, and reclaim 90% of this contribution as a tax credit. They may bear the remaining 10% themselves, or else an independent third party can make up this 10% difference to the LO.

LCF grants can be made to charities or community organisations seeking to create or improve community facilities, heritage and environmental projects. These are categorised by the LCF, but LOs are not required to support all the above categories.

LOs also stipulate that projects must be within a certain distance (typically 5 or 10 miles) of:
- A landfill site which the LO whose funding is being sought manages itself;
- A landfill site managed by any LO;
- A plant which is not a landfill site, but which is involved in waste disposal or processing and is managed by the LO whose funding is being sought.

Once a major source of charity funding, the reduction in land filling since 1996 has led to a corresponding reduction in landfill tax being paid by LOs- and therefore LCF grants. However, for those charities running projects of community value near landfill sites – e.g. the building, improving or expansion of school sports halls, village halls and church halls – the LCF remains a useful source of funding.

Formerly charities could also apply for grants to the Aggregates Levy Sustainability Fund - the equivalent of the LCF for quarrying companies – if they were within a given distance of an active or closed quarry. However, this fund which was started in 2002 was closed by Defra at the end of March 2011.

The National Lottery

The current National Lottery started in 1994. However, it is not a new concept either in the UK or globally.

England first started a National Lottery in 1568. Many important building projects were financed by the National Lottery including almost all the major bridges over the Thames in London. This National Lottery was closed in 1826, following widespread and illegal betting on its outcome.

Today the National Lottery is run by a commercial organisation (at present Camelot plc) on behalf of the government. There are currently 12 lottery funders:

- Arts Council England;
- Arts Council of Northern Ireland;
- Arts Council of Wales;
- British Film Institute;
- Big Lottery Fund;
- Creative Scotland;
- Heritage Lottery Fund;
- Sports England;
- Sport Northern Ireland;
- Sport Wales;
- Sportscotland;
- UK Sport.

Big Lottery Fund (formerly known as the Communities Fund) is the fund of greatest interest to small charities, as their long-term programmes (e.g. Reaching Communities) and time-limited programmes cover a range of charitable areas.

Some 28% of National Lottery proceeds go to good causes (not necessarily registered charities). 50% goes in prizes, 12% in tax and 10% in operating costs.

Key points about funding from the National Lottery are as follows:

- Some programmes are UK-wide; whilst others are applicable only in England or Wales or Scotland or Northern Ireland;
- Lottery funding is available to a wide range of voluntary and community organisations, and not just to registered charities. For example, local councils can bid for lottery funding;
- Lottery providers major on 'outcomes'. This word and the concepts behind it are not always universally understood, and a brief clarification is at the end of this chapter in Appendix A;
- Lottery applications have been simplified in recent years, but they are still long and complex, and not easy for the volunteer to complete;
- Most lottery applications take months to process and are therefore often unsuitable where funding is needed quickly;
- The main exception to this is the Awards for All programme. This offers charities and community groups grants of up to £10,000 for one-off projects or pieces of equipment. Turnaround time is usually six weeks. Only £10,000 worth of funding can be sought in any one twelve month period, and projects must be completed or equipment purchased within twelve months of the receipt of a grant.

Your plan should look like this:
- Access the National Lottery website for information about which funders are likely to support your project (www.lotterygoodcauses.org.uk/funding-finder);
- Call the selected funder(s) and discuss your project on the telephone;
- If possible, visit the funder (there are regional offices for each fund throughout the UK) to discuss your project. The advantage of this is that you will speak to an experienced case officer, whereas the telephone helpline staff often have

a limited knowledge of grant programmes and application procedures;

• Draft your funding application and then if possible arrange for a case officer to look at it before you submit it. Failing this, attend one of the many seminars that the different lottery funders and some other organisations provide, so that you can check their advice against what you have written and amend your application accordingly;

• Once you have submitted your application, it is quite likely that officers of the Lottery fund involved or their professional representatives will wish to visit your project. If this is the case, ensure that they receive the 'red carpet' treatment – welcomed at the start, provided with refreshments/meal as appropriate, briefed by knowledgeable volunteers and handed hard copy details of key points. This sounds a blinding glimpse of the obvious, but I have witnessed occasions when volunteers argued with Lottery staff, cold-shouldered them or did no more than merely tolerate their presence. And then they complained because no grant was forthcoming!

• If, as you hope, a grant is made, it is likely to come with conditions including a requirement for reports. Failure to note and action these are likely to ensure that no future grants from that or other lottery funders are approved.

Funds from Europe

Approximately 0.8% of the European Union's total budget is spent on education, culture, social protection and health. This contrasts with some 50% spent on agriculture.

The European Union (EU) does not fund projects which it believes should be funded by member state governments. It sees itself as enabling projects to be undertaken which would be impossible without EU funding, and that EU resources should supplement, rather than replace, resources already allocated at a national level.

The EU is also keen to fund projects which are:
- Innovatory;
- Capable of being replicated in other parts of the EU.

This ensures that EU money spent in one country will benefit people in at least one other member state.

For small UK charities, finding a project which meets these two criteria can be challenging.

The EU has four principal structural funds. Two of these, the European Agricultural Guidance and Guarantee Fund (EAGGF) and the Financial Instrument for Fisheries Guidance (FIFG) are not appropriate for small charity fundraising. The remaining two funds are:
- The European Regional Development Fund (ERDF);
- The European Social Fund (ESF).

The ERDF aims to reduce imbalances in the economies of different areas and to support deprived rural and industrial areas. The fund will finance both capital and revenue costs.

The ESF supports training, learning and guidance projects to enable people to play a more active role in the economy. In general, the ESF will fund only revenue costs, e.g. salaries, the hire of buildings, heating costs etc. It will not fund large capital costs such as the purchase of land or buildings.

Certain areas of the UK (designated Objective 1) are more likely to receive EU funding owing to their perceived economic problems. These areas are Cornwall and the Isles of Scilly; Merseyside; South Yorkshire; West Wales and the Valleys.

It can be seen that securing funds from the EU for a small charity providing services in a local area will be challenging. Furthermore, the preparation of the submission and the timeframe in which it will be considered are too long for all small charities but those who are engaged in long term planning.

Your plan should look like this:
- Research EU current funding programmes and see where your project might fit in;

- Consider whether project is unique and/or has benefit to communities in other EU countries;
- Find out more about selected programme(s) from contact address;
- Check on town twinning links, if appropriate;
- Discuss with EU funding officer at your county council or unitary authority and enlist council support for funding bid;
- If your county council or unitary authority has a Brussels office, arrange to visit or meet representative in UK;
- Write up your project funding submission;
- Get your MEP on board and ensure he/she sends letter of support.

Checklist

Statutory funding – national government
- Check Government funding website;
- Eliminate Departments/Ministries unlikely to fund your project;
- Narrow down programmes by appropriate Departments;
- Call Departments to discuss proposed submission.

Statutory Funding – local government
- Is your charity in 3 tier or unitary authority?
- Check council funding programmes;
- Read through Strategic Plan;
- Provide services council(s) want;
- Discusse with council officer(s);
- Funding from Town or Parish;
- Mayor/Chairman's chosen charity;
- Councillors' Empowerment Fund.

National Lottery
- Check National Lottery website;

- Choose funders(s) likely to fund your project;
- Discuss with lottery case officer;
- Draft submission, check with case officer or attend seminar;
- Plan Lottery officer visit where appropriate.

Funds from Europe
- Research current funding programmes;
- Is your project innovatory or capable of replication?
- Twinning links;
- Discuss with Council EU funding officer;
- Meet Council Brussels representative, if applicable;
- Draft submission;
- MEP on board.

Appendix A: DEMONSTRATING OUTCOMES

Local authorities and the National Lottery set great store by 'Outcomes'. But what do they mean? And how do you arrive at them? Outcomes are a feature of results-based management approach – much favoured by funders since they show that funds granted to a charity contribute to the achievement of clearly stated results. This approach has four levels:

Inputs
The resources and methods employed to conduct an activity, project or programme. Inputs can be human (e.g labour costs); physical (e.g. equipment purchase); or material (e.g. supplies). Processes are the methods or courses of action selected to conduct the work, e.g. training, capacity building or service provision.

Outputs
These relate to the completion of activities and reflect the intended result from a particular input.

Outcomes
These are the changes and effects that happen as a result of your charity's project. They answer the 'so what?' question and are in effect all the changes and effects that occur as a result of your charity's work.

Impact
Changes which are broader and longer-term than outcomes, resulting from the aims and implementation of your charity's project.

To demonstrate Outcomes to funders, you need to explain what positive changes and beneficial effects will take place if the project you are asking them to fund goes ahead with their support.

Chapter 7: Corporate donors

There is never a good time for corporate fundraising. This is particularly the case where small charities are concerned. In a recession, companies never have any cash to spare; and in a boom time they never have any cash to spare because they are saving against the next recession. This is a slightly cynical view but one which has more than a grain of truth in it!

Charity giving is, of course, supposed to be altruistic. Our only reward is the warm glow of having given to a worthwhile cause or having benefited those less fortunate than we are. Companies, however, expect some good publicity and their names up in neon lights, which is why they tend to support the big national charities rather than small ones like yours.

But all is not lost. Whether you live in or near a small country town or a major city, corporate donors are a potential source of funding you can't afford to ignore. As always in fundraising, you need to start with a clear plan.

Why do companies give?

Since the middle of the 19th century, there have always been large corporate philanthropists like Lord Leverhulme and Lord Nuffield. Not only did they give huge sums to charity during their lifetimes, but the trusts and foundations they set up continue to be generous supporters of a variety of charitable projects.

Corporate giving changed during the second half of the 20th century and moved from being purely philanthropic to become to a greater or lesser extent an arm of companies' strategic operations. Companies seek to enter into what is called a 'corporate partnership', where the company supplies the money, skills or other resources to help further the charity's work – and the company's aims.

Companies now more and more look for opportunities for charitable giving which will serve their own aims as well as those of the charities. The websites of all major companies now include pages on 'corporate responsibility' or 'social responsibility' – because they wish to impress on the public that they are not simply interested in making money: they seek to make the world a better place too. Some corporate and social responsibility programmes are more believable than others!

What does this mean for your small charity? Sadly, it is unlikely that the major players will make you large gifts, since you will be unable to provide the national or international benefits they seek. But all is not lost. Small and Medium size Enterprises (SMEs) and subsidiaries of major companies operating in your town or county may well wish to be seen supporting a local charity, particularly if it is providing services for their active or retired workforce.

Aim

You first need to decide what you want from the companies in your area. The obvious thing is money but there are other options which may be more productive for both your charity and the companies near you. Broadly, the options are:

A cash gift
This will always be challenging as companies do not have much spare cash (or so they say) and your small charity is unlikely to be top of their giving list.

Sponsorship
Sponsorship is different from giving in that the donor receives something tangible in return. For example, if your church is planning to put on a series of fundraising concerts featuring distinguished organists from all over the UK, a company might well sponsor this (i.e. pay all the costs involved) in return for a number of free tickets per concert; the best seats in the church; free

refreshments before, during or after the concert; and their name prominently displayed on the concert programmes. Sponsorship comes in other forms: your local supermarket might provide all the food and wine free of charge in exchange for appropriate publicity. The advantage of sponsorship is that with all the costs taken care of, your entire income from ticket sales will go to your charitable activities and even if few attend your event, you will not end up with a financial loss.

Gifts in kind

Imagine your school is raising funds for a new sports hall. If you can persuade a building supply firm to provide all the bricks free of charge or even at cost, you will have scored a major coup. The bricks might have cost your school £200,000: if this firm donates them, it will have made a gift worth £200,000 to you (i.e. £200,000 cash which you have not had to raise), but may only cost the firm £90,000. The firm receives the kudos of a £200,000 gift which has only cost it £90,000 whilst your school has all the bricks needed for the sports hall without having to raise the funds – probably from many different donors – to purchase them. Everyone is a winner!

Items for fundraising events

If you are coming towards the end of your fundraising campaign, you may be able to persuade local companies to donate prizes for your competitions, raffles and tombolas – particularly if they manufacture or sell something likely to be attractive, such as holidays, meals at smart restaurants, fine wines or bespoke menswear and womenswear.

Remember though that you have to explain to companies what is in it for them – unless you know that they have an established track record for supporting your charitable activity. You can still be tough though. Some years ago, I was directing a capital fundraising campaign for a high profile hospice. The manager of the local branch of a well-known supermarket offered me a handful of his supermarket's vouchers. I was duly grateful – but asked him if he knew of any construction firms which would accept payment in these vouchers. He got the message: the vouchers were replaced by a larger – and cash – donation!

Which firms might give?

The best start points are:
- Your local Chamber of Commerce and Industry. Most local companies will belong to this, and if the Chamber has a sympathetic chief executive or, better still, some of your volunteers are members, you can usually get access to their database free of charge. You will then have the names of all your local companies at your fingertips, together with much other useful detail;
- Kompass. Formerly available in book form, this is an on-line service designed to put businesses in touch with each other. It will list all the companies in your local town by size and business type, together with their owners or boards of management, turnover and contact details. This will enable you to see not only which companies might have funds to spare for your project, but also which ones have business in-terests which might complement those of your charity.

Persuade one or more of your volunteers to study the local press on a daily or weekly basis, as appropriate. This will give you in-formation about the activities of local companies, especially:
- Any big and profitable orders they have landed;
- Their support for charities in general, and the types of charities that interest them.

The List

Your next task will be to shortlist the companies in your area. You can achieve this by taking into account a number of factors and seeing how many companies match one or more of these. Questions you need to ask include:

- Does the company have a track record of charitable giving?
- Has the company been especially profitable in recent years?
- Does the company manufacture or sell goods or services applicable to our charity in general or the current fundraising campaign in particular?
- Do any of our volunteers or supporters own the company or serve on its board of management?
- Do any of our volunteers or supporters know company owners or directors?
- Does the company encourage its workforce to become involved in charitable and voluntary activities?

The more 'ticks in the boxes' a company receives from your research, the better chance you have of securing their support in one form or another.

Preparing 'The Ask'

You've shortlisted your local companies. Now you need to find out how to reach the point of being able to ask for their support. You will need to discover:

- Who makes the decisions about the company's charitable giving. The Board of Management? A Director or Manager assigned to that role? Or is a vote taken across the whole workforce?
- Is there a 'Charity of the Year'? If so, you will need to find out when this is chosen for the next year and be prepared to fight your corner!
- Does the company 'match' any gift made by the workforce? Even small workforces may raise five figure sums and, for example, a £15,000 sum raised by the workforce and then

matched £1 for £1 by the management will result in a substantial donation;

•   Are there any national schemes which might be applicable? For example, Sportsmatch is a national scheme where Sport England will match fund donations by companies (and some other funders) for eligible grassroots sports activities in England;

•   How do you get in front of the decision maker(s)? Do you need to recruit a sympathetic 'champion' who will persuade the Board to listen to your presentation? Or do you need to book up a slot when the workforce next assembles to listen to words of wisdom about the company's future?

Once you know who you have to convince and on what occasion, you can then set about preparing a presentation of the right length and in appropriate depth for your audience, whatever size and level that may be.

Remember though that unlike grant-making trusts, companies do not exist to support charities like yours. So you will have to make a strong case for support even if there are no other local charities competing for funds.

Continuing relationships

Many grant-making trusts are happy to support small charities on a regular basis, and often only expect an annual letter requesting funds – although some do insist of project reports.

Companies have many other commitments, and unless you cement the relationship and continue to reinforce it, you will find that out of sight is very much out of mind. Once you have secured your donation, gift in kind or sponsorship, try and get supporting companies involved on a long-term basis. This can be achieved in a number of ways:

•   Inviting a senior member of the company to be a Trustee, or possibly a Patron of your charity;

• Encouraging a scheme in which volunteers from the company can undertake work with your charity. This does not only offer the opportunity to benefit from skilled labour free of charge, but it will cement in the volunteers' mind the value of what your charity is doing and encourage them to support it – or persuade the company to support it – in the longer term;

• Proposing to the Board of Management that they initiate a Payroll Giving scheme to benefit your charity. Payroll giving is a highly effective method of securing a regular monthly income for your charity whilst not creating a large extra administrative burden for the participating company. It has the additional advantage of needing little continuing input from your charity except regularly to thank participants and ask them to increase their giving from time to time. Payroll giving is discussed in greater detail in Chapter 9 (p.143).

But be warned: companies increasingly expect their charitable causes to be run like businesses and, alongside meeting targets and delivering results, they will be expected to have a positive impact on company profits. Quite simply, their expenditure in both time and money will have to yield tangible results.

So, when you are seeking corporate donations and, especially, a longer term relationship, always 'think business'. Ask yourself: 'what's it in for them?' If you can get that right, you are in with a reasonable chance of success.

Checklist

Aim
- Identify corporate support you are looking for;
- Cash;
- Sponsorship;
- Gifts in kind;
- Items for fundraising events;
- More than one of the above.

Check out the firms
- Research in Kompass and/or Chamber of Commerce;
- Volunteers to check local media for firms' successful contracts and their charity giving track record;
- Full list of details – owners/directors, turnover, business type, contact details;
- Opportunities for gifts in kind.

Listing the firms
- Charitable giving track record;
- Recent profitability;
- Goods or services applicable to our charity/current project;
- Charity volunteers on boards of management;
- Charity volunteers' contacts with boards of management;
- Workforce encouraged to become involved in local charities.

The Ask
- Identify who makes decisions on charitable giving;
- Is there a 'Charity of the Year'? Find the procedure;
- Company 'match' sums raised by the workforce;
- National schemes which might be applicable/attractive;
- Find out how to get to the decision-makers;
- Identify the audience for your presentation.

Continuing relationships
- Identify ways to keep the companies on board in the longer term;
- Directors as Trustees/Patrons;
- Workforce volunteer on regular basis or for specific projects;
- Continuing the financial support, e.g. payroll giving;
- What's in it for them?

Chapter 8: Wealthy individuals

It is often said that charity fundraising is all about people. People give to people; they do not give to causes. People usually give because the person asking them is someone they like or admire or to whom they owe a favour.

Wealthy individuals therefore represent a key target for your small charity. The only problem is that most wealthy people are wealthy because they hang on to their money!

If your charity happens to have a Trustee or volunteer who has made their millions, then this is a great advantage. But for the majority of small charities, finding individual major donors (or high net worth (HNW) individuals, as they are sometimes called) will be the result of long and painstaking research. This research will involve all of your volunteers and supporters, to a greater or lesser extent.

The research will initially follow two simultaneous and parallel lines: one to identify well-known wealthy individuals who might be persuaded to give to your campaign (celebrities and the 'great & good'); and the other to identify wealthy individuals who are not well-known and keep a low profile – to the extent that their wealth may only be apparent to a small number of close friends and business associates.

Celebrities and the 'Great & Good'

Celebrities are essentially successful people who have a high public profile and have made considerable sums of money during their working lives. Very often they will have experiences or circumstances which potentially link them to particular charitable activities. For example, a celebrity who has spent time in an inner city area working for homeless people might be interested in supporting a project to help homeless people in your town find full-time jobs and permanent accommodation. Another celebrity with a grandchild who has autistic spectrum disorder (ASD) might be attracted to a charity working with autistic children. The wealth of these celebrities is often referred to as 'new money'.

The 'Great & Good' are more likely to be people who have inherited money. They are often high profile, particularly in their own locality, and are well-known because their families have a tradition of public service. They hold traditional and largely unpaid posts like those of Lord Lieutenant and Deputy Lieutenant (DL); High Sheriff; and sometimes Justice of the Peace (JP). Many have their own family trusts, or the positions they hold have funds supported by the taxpayer. Their wealth is known as 'old money'.

Initial research

Celebrities can be researched on Google and other search engines using your charity's geographical area and the activities in which your charity is engaged. So, if you are raising funds for your church, you should be able to come up with a list of celebrities who live in your county or unitary authority area and are practising Christians or enthusiasts for heritage buildings, or both. It is probably not worth identifying celebrities outside your county boundaries, unless your charity is in one authority area but provides services in another authority area close by.

The 'Great & Good' are more effectively researched through more traditional sources. Each County or authority with a Lord Lieutenant has a Lieutenancy Office. Frequently these are co-located with County Hall. A call to the Lieutenancy Office should produce a list of names of the Lord Lieutenant, Vice Lord Lieutenant and Deputy Lieutenants – although some Lieutenancy Offices can be very coy about supplying names, let alone full contact details, despite the fact that the names at least are in the public domain. County Hall will also be able to offer the best way of contacting the High Sheriff.

Who's Who and Debrett's *Distinguished People of Today* are useful sources of information for both celebrities and the 'Great & Good'. Most major libraries have both these publications in CD-ROM form in their reference sections, and this will allow far quicker and more effective research than the book forms of both publications offer. In particular, by entering the name of your town or village, the CD-ROM version will provide a list of everyone in the publication who has included that town or village in their biographical details. Sometimes this information is not helpful, and I recall on one occasion a celebrity whose connection with the town in question was simply that he had married a woman from there – whom he had later divorced. Not a very likely prospect! However, the same research came up with a distinguished academic brought up and educated in the town, but now living in New South Wales. I wrote to him and he sent a handsome donation to the fundraising campaign.

There are other biographical volumes such as *The International Authors' and Writers' Who's Who* and *The Blue Book*, together with a variety of on-line websites which provide details about celebrities and other potential donors.

In April each year, the *Sunday Times* produces its Rich List of the 1,000 wealthiest people or families in the UK. It is available in hard copy, and also on-line – register for the on-line version on www.timesplus.co.uk.

There are other lists of rich and influential people covering specific regions (e.g. *The Birmingham Post's* 'Midlands' Rich List' – www.birminghampost.net) or spheres of life (e.g. *The Guardian's* 'The Guardian Media 100' – www.guardian.co.uk – and *The Evening Standard's* 'London's 1,000 Most Influential People' – www.standard.co.uk). Hemscott Company Guru provides information on company directors – www.hemscott.com/guru.

Next steps

Evaluation

Now that you have a shortlist of celebrities and 'Great & Good' who might be persuaded to support your campaign, your next step is to organise a focus group of volunteers to give their opinions on the names you have produced.

You may already have touched on this process when you set up your Campaign Management Team and evaluated donors and 'ambassadors', but your focus group will concentrate on wealthy individual donors and set in place concrete plans for approaching them. This is the point at which the 'unknown' wealthy are brought into the equation. You will be looking not only at the wealth of these individuals, but also their track record of giving; connections they may have with your charity and its activities; whether they might in addition give the charity support in other ways; and – most importantly – the person(s) best placed to approach them.

An *aide mémoire* for evaluating individual donors is at Appendix A to this chapter.

Training

Few people find it easy to ask for gifts, even if they are asking someone they know well and on behalf of a charitable cause from which they will derive no personal benefit. So it is important to brief and train your focus group (and any other volunteers you may involve in asking for gifts). Knowledge dispels fear!

Following your focus group meeting, organise training session which should include:

1. The preparation necessary for an 'ask'.
2. What the 'asker' needs to do and say at the meeting.
3. The follow-up to the 'ask'.
4. Consideration should be given to including a 'playlet' where the right and wrong ways of conducting an 'ask' are illustrated.

An *aide mémoire* for training your volunteers in a personal approach is at Appendix B to this chapter. An *aide mémoire* for undertaking a personal approach is an Appendix C to this chapter.

Receptions
Asking each major donor individually for a gift is a time-consuming business. It is worth the effort when a large donation is expected – and even more so when that donation arrives!

However, there are likely to be a number of potential donors who might give three figure or possibly even four figure sums. If the number is large, you are unlikely to find sufficient volunteers with the time to ask each one individually for a gift.

Where this is the case, a drinks reception or informal supper party achieves the necessary personal touch for a group ask to be made, whilst at the same time allowing one or a small number of volunteers to seek gifts from a substantial number of potential donors on a single occasion.

An *aide mémoire* for organising a reception or small supper is at Appendix D to this chapter.

Checklist

Celebrity search
- Google celebrities with links to your geographical area;
- Google celebrities with links to/interests in your charity's activities;
- Locate major library with *Who's Who* and Debrett's on CD-ROM;
- Consider alternative sources – books and on-line.

'Great & Good' search
- Contact Office of the Lieutenancy;
- Contact High Sheriff's Office/County Hall;
- Check details in *Who's Who* and Debrett's;
- Consider alternative sources – books and on-line.

Wealthy Individuals Focus Group - Plans
- Shortlist suitable members from amongst your volunteers;
- Invite 6-12 volunteers to form focus group;
- Appoint Chairman of focus group;
- Recruit volunteer secretary for group;
- Agree venue with Chairman;
- E-mail selection of dates/times for members at least 6 weeks before meeting;
- E-mail members one week before meeting with central list of celebrities and 'Great & Good' and ask members to bring their own lists of 'unknown' wealthy;
- Send directions to venue and confirm attendance with all;
- Visit venue beforehand and check administration – meeting room, refreshments etc.

Wealthy Individuals Focus Group – Meeting
- Chairman to thank all for attending and declare 'Chatham House Rule';
- Volunteer secretary has chart with key details;
- Chairman to ensure meeting keeps to time and that all views on prospects are heard;
- Secretary collates views and plan, and circulates to all members after meeting.

Training session
- Agree date with volunteers;
- Organise venue with refreshments;
- Organise video recording equipment;
- Organise interviewer;
- Arrange three volunteers to act out 'playlet';
- Organise paperwork for volunteers attending.

Appendix A: EVALUATING INDIVIDUAL DONORS AND OTHER KEY SUPPORTERS

It is essential for the success of your fundraising campaign that you identify early in the campaign process potential individual donors, and other personalities who will benefit the campaign through raising its profile or influencing those who might be persuaded to lend their support.

To ensure that no potential donors or supporter is over-looked, you need to organise a focus group to carry out one or more evaluation meetings. These meetings will be informal gatherings round the table, but will have formal notes prepared by the focus group secretary.

The nucleus of the evaluation focus group will probably be the Campaign Management Team. However, it will often be useful to invite other volunteers to take part, or to set up a series of evaluation meetings with different volunteers on the focus group to cover specific geographical or business areas.

The evaluation meetings are set up to achieve the following:
•   Identify likely donors to your campaign;
•   Identify other supporters who will act as 'ambassadors' and promote the campaign publicly;
•   Decide who amongst the CMT and other campaign volunteers will approach these individuals for their support.

Your initial focus group meeting should be organised along these lines:

Preparation:
•   Recruit volunteers to your focus group (at least 6; no more than 12) who ideally have wide-ranging social and/or business contacts, or who have lived in your locality for many years;

- Select a Chairman who is positive, persuasive and able to motivate willing volunteers who nonetheless need encouragement and support; and an effective secretary for the group. The latter might well be your Campaign Secretary;
- Choose a venue which is easy to find and access, and where there is sufficient on- and off-street parking. Ideally, this should be the home of the Chairman;
- Plan a selection of dates and times with the Chairman at least 6 weeks' ahead to maximise the chances of the whole focus group being able to attend;
- A week before the meeting, send out your list of celebrities and the 'Great & Good', asking all members of the focus group to think about the names and anyone who might be connected with them, and requesting them to be prepared to give an opinion about any they know, or know of, and their likely support for your charity;
- In the same letter, ask each volunteer to bring a list of names of people who are not on your list, but are wealthy and might be persuaded to give;
- Send out directions to the venue and confirm that everyone who initially said they would attend is in fact going to do so;
- Visit the venue several days in advance and ensure that there is a suitable room with appropriate seating arrangements (ideally the focus group will be seated at a table) and that refreshments will be provided (if necessary at the charity's expense).

The meeting:
- The initial meeting should last no more than 1.5 hours; one hour is probably ideal;
- The Chairman should not only thank all attending for giving up their time, but should also declare 'Chatham House Rule', so that focus group members are enabled to give an unvarnished view about the likelihood of those individuals

being discussed giving to the campaign, without comments being passed back to the individuals concerned;

• The volunteer secretary should prepare a chart which she/he can fill in during the meeting and then circulate to the focus group after the meeting. This will need to show at the least the names of potential donors; which members of the focus group suggested them; and who is best placed to approach the targets for a gift (usually – but not always – the person suggesting them). It is also helpful for the person who proposes a name or knows a name already proposed to score each one in terms of their knowledge of them. So, for example, those scored 'A' will be known to the proposer or another focus group member 'very well indeed'; those 'B' will be 'quite well known'; and those 'C' 'nodding acquaintance only';

• At the meeting, the Chairman will need to exercise firm 'grip' – first, to ensure that the time limit agreed is adhered to; and secondly, to allow each member of the focus group to comment on the central looks of names as well as put forward their own list and comment on the names put forward by other group members;

• At the end of the meeting, you should have ended up with a list of potential major donors together with a graded ('A' to 'C') list of those on the focus group who might approach them for a gift;

• You are also likely to have a list of possible 'ambassadors' who will donate at a lower level than the potential major donors, but in addition support the campaign in other ways;

After the evaluation meeting the focus group secretary should produce a chart, showing the names of those evaluated by category; and who is to approach each individual listed. This list should also include deadlines for action.

Once approaches have been made, gifts solicited and 'ambassadors' recruited, consideration should be given to holding further evaluation meetings both to review progress with existing approaches and to consider new approaches. The focus group secretary is the crucial conduit of information and mutual support between the CMT and those approaching donors and other personalities.

Appendix B: ORGANISING A TRAINING SESSION

A small charity is only likely to have one opportunity to seek a major gift from any one wealthy individual. So it is critical that the 'ask' is effective as this will maximise the chances of success.

The key issue is that the 'ask' must take place face-to-face. In the United Kingdom, volunteers will go to almost any lengths to avoid this, preferring the letter or telephone. Every study and statistic on fundraising ever produced shows that letters to wealthy individuals produce negligible results, and telephone calls are scarcely any more effective. Nonetheless, many volunteers persist with these 2 media, offering a raft of excuses as to why they cannot undertake a personal meeting instead.

It is of course obvious that a face-to-face meeting is much more time-consuming than writing a letter or making a telephone call – but the dividends far outweigh the extra time committed, assuming of course that the right wealthy individuals are targeted in the first place.

Most of us feel awkward asking others for money, even though it is not for ourselves or for any activity from which we will personally benefit. So an informal training session (no more than half a day) will assist the inexperienced or doubtful in making the most of their personal 'ask' meetings. Such a session can be organised with minimum cost and work.

Preliminaries
- Ensure all attending the session have received key information about the fundraising campaign, and ask them to attend having briefed themselves fully on the key aspects of the campaign;
- Organise a venue with refreshments;
- Organise video recording equipment;
- Organise an interviewer – local journalist?
- Find 3 volunteers (e.g. members of village amateur dramatics) who can perform a simple 'playlet'.

The 'Playlet'

A simple 'playlet' should bring home to the audience the effectiveness of a personal ask over writing or telephoning.

- Scene 1. An office with busy CEO and PA. PA brings in begging letter from friend of CEO. CEO dismisses this as yet another request for funds and throws it into the waste paper bin. A few moments later, the telephone rings. PA answers and tells CEO that it is Mr X on a 'confidential matter'. CEO laughs and says Mr X only wants money for something, and tells PA to say that he is in a meeting/out/unwell;

- Scene 2. Charity volunteer arrives at office for an agreed meeting, and is admitted by PA. CEO tries to be off-putting by claiming that he is very busy or needs to keep up with the Test Match score. Volunteer is polite but firm and promises he/she won't waste CEO's time. After a short summary of the campaign and its aims and objectives, volunteer answers questions put by CEO. CEO then either agrees to make a gift then and there, or asks for time to consider. In the latter case volunteer insists on deadline for this when he will call CEO. Meeting ends with usual farewells.

Programme

- After tea/coffee, invite the students to sit down to watch the playlet;

- After playlet, students are interviewed on video. First session involves them simply talking about themselves. This is something most people can do quite easily, and it therefore reduces nervousness and boosts confidence;

- Second session is an interview about the campaign. This will get the students talking easily and knowledgeably about the fundraising campaign and answering likely questions;

- After break, students participate in round-table discussion about their performances on video and any outstanding points are covered and questions answered;

- Students depart with all the printed information they need for their 'ask' sessions.

Questions likely to be asked by wealthy individuals and for use in training sessions

Q1. Why are you having a fundraising campaign? Why doesn't the County Council/Diocese/other organisation pay?

A1. The County Council/Diocese has generously supported our fundraising campaign, but it has other calls on its limited resources. In addition to the County Council/Diocese, every parent and member of staff/every adult member of our congregation has given, and as a result we have raised $£x$ towards our $£y$ target. But we need your support to bridge our $£z$ gap and therefore reach our target.

Q2. I have given to your charity in the past - why me again?

A2. You must be thrilled with what we have achieved for our community/homeless people/children with disabilities in the past, and will surely want to see us improve and expand what we are able to provide so that more people will benefit from our charitable work.

Q3. Your charity's building looks all right to me.

A3. Appearances deceive. It is suffering from wet and dry rot, and needs major conservation and refurbishment, otherwise it will soon be unsafe for public use. There is no building of similar size in the village, so the whole village will lose out if the building deteriorates to an unsafe condition.

Q4. I'm not a member of your charity, so why should I give?

A4. Of course our fundraising campaign will specifically benefit those who need to access our charity's services. But our project will also have a much wider community benefit, providing volunteering opportunities for young and old alike, including those with disabilities.

Q5. My company will make a substantial donation if you give us the building (or other….) contract.

A5. Our Trustees have decided to put the contracts out to tender. It would clearly be unethical for our charity to accept a gift if it appeared that the tendering process became a sham as a result.

Q6. I don't want to make a gift which will simply be absorbed into the general project.

A6. That's not a problem. We have prepared a list of designated gifts, so that those who wish to make a donation for a specific part of the project or items of fittings or equipment may do so, and in some cases have these items named after them or some one else of their choice.

Q7. What happens if you raise more than is needed? What will happen to the surplus?

A7. That will be the Trustees' decision. However, it seems likely that they would wish to create a sustainability fund so that our charity and its work in the community can be assured for many years to come.

Q8. What happens if you don't achieve your target?

A8. We intend to achieve the target. We have costed our Campaign project, and our Trustees have assessed the feasibility of raising our target. But we do need your help to ensure we succeed in the timeframe the Trustees have published.

Appendix C: UNDERTAKING A PERSONAL APPROACH TO WEALTHY INDIVIDUALS

Key points

It has been shown conclusively over very many years that the most effective way of eliciting gifts is to ask the potential donor face-to-face. Unfortunately, this flies in the face of the British psyche: most Britons would much rather write a letter or, at best, make a telephone call although these 2 methods have been shown to be far less effective than a face-to-face meeting.

This is of course the counsel of perfection. In reality, the potential donors may outnumber the asking volunteers to such an extent that the one-to-one meetings necessary would represent an impossibly large task. For this reason, one-to-one meetings are suitable only when the donor is very well known to the asker and the potential for a very substantial gift is great.

Alternative options are large receptions (for 50-100 guests) or small lunch or supper parties for fewer than 50 guests. The more personal an approach, the more effective it will be - the less personal, the less effective.

1. *Preparations*
   - Read/watch and understand the campaign literature, briefing notes or DVD provided;
   - Telephone your 'prospect' first - 'I want to come and see you to talk about something I believe is very important and which I think you will find interesting also';
   - Arrange to see them 'within the next few days';
   - Do not discuss the matter on the telephone - 'I will tell you when I see you';
   - DO NOT put the literature or DVD in the post before the meeting. Take it/them along to the meeting;
   - Avoid writing - however much your prospect asks you to because he/she is too busy to see you. If he/she won't see you, then you have chosen the wrong person!

• Even if you only see your prospect for 5 minutes, he/she will be impressed by your insistence that you should, and with the trouble you have taken. They will begin to feel obliged to you - the start of the giving process;

• Take with you a supply of literature items both for your own reference and that you can leave with your prospect.

2. *The meeting*

• Explain your involvement, that you feel the charity in general and its current fundraising campaign in particular deserves your commitment, and the intended project(s). Explain that the charity's volunteers are approaching influential, committed people whom the charity feels will wish to make major gifts to the Campaign which are essential if it is to succeed;

• Point out that major gifts for specific pieces of work – e.g. a particular room in the church complex - can be associated with donors' names;

• Emphasise the importance of the fundraising project to the community at large. This is especially important if your charity is a school or church where there may be a public perception that the only beneficiaries will be those most closely involved – church worshippers, staff and parents, residents of a narrowly defined area;

• Leave a copy or copies of appropriate literature behind;

• Before you leave, express the hope that he/she will wish to support your fundraising campaign as generously as possible, and say that you will be in touch in a specific timeframe (e.g. one week). This is essential.

3. *Follow up*

• Send a brief thank you note immediately after the meeting, again expressing the hope that they will give. Make a judgment as to whether this should be a letter, or if an e-mail will be sufficient;

- At the end of the agreed period of time, if no response has been received, follow up again by telephone asking whether they have come to a decision;
- Once a gift has been received, send a further letter of thanks and make sure that the Chairman of your charity also writes in their official capacity.

Appendix D (i): ORGANISING FUNDRAISING RECEPTIONS

1.   A small fundraising lunch/supper or a larger drinks reception is much less intimate than a one-to-one meeting – but both require at least as much preparation and organisation.

2.   Choose a location which can be located easily by guests, including those who do not have SATNAVs. Ensure there is the necessary parking and appropriate entertainment facilities for the numbers expected.

3.   Don't choose a date which clashes with some popular local or national event.

4.   As soon as you fix your date, consider telephoning your planned guests or sending them 'save the date' e-mails/cards so that they have your event firmly in their diaries and that your formal invitation arrives as confirmation of an occasion of which they are already aware and likely to accept.

5.   Send out invitations at least 8 weeks in advance. Then, if response is less positive than expected, you will have time to invite the 'second team' without it being obvious to them that this is the case.

6.   Make it clear that this is a fundraising event. People are unlikely to give if they feel they have been invited under false pretences.

7.   Ensure all your costs – venue hire, catering, drinks – are sponsored; and tell your guests that this is so. Avoid if possible paying any costs out of the funds already raised for the campaign.

8.	Give your guests a drink – then tell them all about your fundraising campaign early on in the proceedings. After that, let them enjoy themselves! If they have had a good night out, they will be in a better frame of mind to give.

9.	Make sure your guests have appropriate literature to take away – but preferably do not give it to them until they are leaving. This will reduce the possibility of guests leaving the literature behind.

10.	Follow up – this is essential. For those who give 'on the night', send a thank you letter (not e-mail) within 48 hours. For those who do not, a telephone call after a fortnight if they have still not given; and a letter a fortnight after that. If none of this elicits a gift, they probably aren't going to donate.

11.	A sample follow-up letter is on the following page.

Appendix D (ii): FUNDRAISING RECEPTIONS SAMPLE FOLLOW-UP LETTER

Date

Mr and Mrs A N Other
1 Any Street
Any Town
Anyshire AA1 1AA

Dear

Victoria and I much enjoyed seeing you for supper on 20 May. It was very good to have the pleasure of your company, and we hope that you found the evening pleasant too.

You may remember that I mentioned that the Littlevillage Guildhall Trust Campaign target is £2.1 million. The Campaign's aim is to have achieved £1 million of this by the end of this year, and I am glad to say that we are well on track with almost £650,000 raised so far.

Despite this success, we still have some £250,000 to find if the Campaign is to reach this interim milestone on schedule. So if you have decided to support the Campaign, it would be tremendously helpful if you could let the Campaign Office have your gift by the end of July.

I hope you will forgive me writing so comparatively soon after the supper party, but we are all very keen to help the Campaign reach its target within the timeframe the Chairman of the Campaign Management Team has set.

With very best wishes,

Peter

Chapter 9: Tax-efficient giving

Tax-efficient giving is a well-used buzzphrase in charity fund-raising – but often that is as far as it goes! A large number of small charities throughout the UK fail to take up the benefits of the different schemes available. Tax-efficient giving allows charities to reclaim tax which donors have already paid and allows donors to offset their giving against tax, thereby making a gift to your charity cheaper for them.

Substantial sums are lost by charities each year because they do not take advantage of these schemes or encourage donors to do so. Make sure yours isn't one of those!

Gift Aid

Gift Aid is the best known form of tax-efficient giving. Introduced in 1990, it was originally limited to one-off cash gifts of £600 or more. In 2000 it was extended to include donations of any size and its scope was increased so that donors who wanted to give sums regularly by standing order or direct debit could also utilise this provision.

Gift Aid allows charities to reclaim on any sum given them by a UK taxpayer the basic rate tax which the donor has already paid. Thus on a gift of £50 where the basic rate is 22%, the charity can claim £14.10 in tax, increasing the value of the gift to £64.10.

Donors who are higher rate taxpayers can claim for themselves the difference between the higher and lower rates. So if the basic rate is 22% and the higher rate 40%, a higher rate taxpayer could make a gift of £780 to a charity which would be worth £1,000 to the charity (through reclaim of basic tax) but only cost the higher rate taxpayer £600 (through reclaiming the difference between the higher and basic rates, i.e. 18%).

This means that a gift of any size will actually cost a higher rate taxpayer less than it will cost a basic rate taxpayer. Pro-active charities will encourage higher rate taxpayers to make a larger gift by donating in addition the 18% higher rate relief.

Donors do not have to be resident in the UK to give tax efficiently. However, they do need to pay UK income tax. Charities can only claim Gift Aid on gifts to the level of tax actually paid that year by the donor.

One of the shortcomings of Gift Aid bemoaned by treasurers of small charities was that Gift Aid could only be reclaimed once a year at the end of the financial year. This created a large amount of work for volunteer treasurers in a short timeframe. In 2010 this was addressed by HMRC, who announced that treasurers would be allowed to reclaim Gift Aid on a monthly basis.

HMRC produces the Gift Aid form which charities must ask donors to sign so that Gift Aid can be reclaimed. This can be downloaded from the HMRC website and an example is at Appendix A to this chapter (www.hmrc.gov.uk/charities).

A further change was introduced in April 2013. This is called the Gift Aid Small Donations Scheme (GASDS). GASDS allow charities and CASCs to apply for Gift Aid-style payments on small donations without the need for Gift Aid declarations.

Key features of the scheme are as follows:

- The term 'small donation' means a donation of £20 or less;
- A 'community buildings' rule allows charities to claim top-up payments on an additional amount of donations up to a value of £5,000 for each of its local groups;
- Charities must match each £1 of GASDS with 10p of Gift Aid donations (the so-called '10% rule');
- Charities must have been registered and claiming Gift Aid for at least 2 years before they can claim on the GASDS scheme.

Covenants

Until the introduction of Gift Aid, covenants were the only means of giving cash sums regularly to registered charities. Covenants are legally binding documents which have to be witnessed. Before the 1990s, covenants could be taken out for a minimum of 4 years and a maximum of 7 years, with payments being made monthly, quarterly or annually. Tax can be reclaimed on covenants in exactly the same way as it is reclaimed on Gift Aid.

The advantage of covenants for donors was that they could spread their giving over extended periods of time, thereby often allowing them to give more than they could have afforded in a lump sum. For charities there was also an advantage, as many banks would lend against future covenant payments. Elderly people could also make provision in their Wills to ensure that their covenants – which would normally cease at their death – would be paid in full out of their estate.

However, the recession and consequent unemployment during the 1990s created a situation where covenantors were unable to keep up payments they had agreed to during boom times. The government therefore extended covenants so that they could be taken out for as short a time as one year, with no maximum; and covenantors were allowed to introduce certain phrases agreed by the Inland Revenue to allow them to exit a covenant early if their circumstances changed in a way they had not foreseen, e.g. they ceased to be in full-time employment as a result of redundancy, collapse of their employing company, etc.

Although this offered donors welcome flexibility, it also made the covenants much less watertight. Charities understandably became reluctant to contest those who might decide to cancel a covenant before it was due to finish.

Companies and partnerships can also take out covenants. However, the value of company covenants to charities has reduced since the Government decided to cease allowing charities to reclaim corporation tax paid. However, companies can still offset their donations through company covenants against tax, so company covenants remain a means of persuading companies to give to charities.

Covenants remain an effective method of promoting longer term, committed giving to charities. However, the increase in the scope of Gift Aid and the need to print and administer covenant forms have reduced their popularity in the 21st century as a vehicle for tax efficient giving.

An example of a covenant is at Appendix B to this chapter.

Gifts of shares

When targeting wealthy donors in particular, the tax advantages of giving shares should form part of any 'ask'. This little known system is probably the most advantageous way of tax-efficient giving open to wealthy individuals.

Gifts to charities of publicly quoted shares are exempt from capital gains tax liability. In addition, the donor is able to claim income tax relief on the current value of the shares.

For example, a higher rate taxpayer donating shares to a charity which were bought for £5,000 but now worth £10,000 could save £2,000 in capital gains tax and £4,000 in income tax relief. The gift worth £10,000 to the charity would therefore cost the donor only £4,000.

Donors must donate the shares themselves, i.e. they cannot sell them and donate the proceeds to the charity if they wish to claim the tax relief above.

The charity has the option of encashing the shares or retaining them to provide income and against future capital needs.

Gifts of assets

Individual donors who are asset rich but cash poor may prefer to give through the direct transfer of assets to a charity, either during their lifetime or in their Wills. Assets such as property and works of art do not incur capital gains tax; and if they form bequests they are free from inheritance tax.

Gifts-in-kind

Corporate donors can choose to support your charity by providing needed goods or services, or by seconding staff to help run your campaign. By donating equipment or trading stock to a charity or CASC, a company can reduce its taxable profits - and therefore the tax it pays.

If a company seconds staff to your charity, e.g. a Campaign Secretary, it can claim tax relief on the costs of employing them. This relief also applies if the staff are volunteering in work time. However, this tax relief is available when staff are working for a charity but not if they are working for a CASC.

Payroll Giving

Despite encouragement by a succession of governments, Payroll Giving remains a greatly under-used method of tax efficient giving.

Reference has been made to this scheme in Chapter 7, but this chapter provides more detail of the scheme and its advantages for small charities.

The key point about payroll giving schemes is that they provide charities with a regular, monthly income. As a vehicle for helping small charities with their running costs and making them more sustainable long-term, payroll giving is excellent. However, it is less effective for a charity wishing to raise a large capital sum in a one-off fundraising appeal.

Over 50% of the UK's working population of 13.2 million are employed by some 4470 businesses with more than 500 employees. Most of these businesses have payroll schemes involving over 0.5 million people.

However, there are nearly 2.4 million Small and Medium size Enterprises (SMEs) in the UK, each employing less than

500 people. Approximately 11.5 million people work for SMEs. Most SMEs do not have payroll giving schemes. This means that there is tremendous potential for initiating payroll giving schemes in SMEs in your town or village.

Payroll Giving Schemes work in the following way:

• Employees decide how much they wish to give monthly and choose a charity to receive this payment;

• Employees in one company do not have to all give to the same charity;

• The employer chooses a Payroll Giving Agency (PGA) to administer the scheme for their company;

• The monthly payments are deducted from the employee's pay at source by the PGA, and then paid to the charity.

The advantages to all parties are as follows:

• There is no cost to the employer as the PGA deducts an agreed amount/percentage from the donations;

• The charity does not have to worry about reclaiming Gift Aid, as the donations are made from pre-tax income;

• The employee does not have to fund charity giving out of his/her net income.

Statistics show that few employees terminate payroll giving schemes, so the long term income is almost guaranteed except in industries with high staff turnover such as hospitality and hairdressing. The role of the PGA is as follows:

• Processes all paperwork;

• Makes a charge for administration – deducted from employees' gifts;

• Provides support to employers and charities in setting up scheme;

• Provides disbursement statements to charities to track donors and payments.

The role of the employer is as follows:
- Signs contract and send to chosen PGA;
- Sends money within 14 days of end of income tax month;
- Provides breakdown of employees' names.

Setting up a Payroll Giving Scheme

Your charity needs to take the following action:
- Select the employer(s) to be targeted;
- Establish a contact within each targeted company (Internal Champion);
- Through Internal Champion liaise with Finance Department, Payroll Manager and HR department;
- Through Internal Champion arrange time to talk to staff – in groups if there are large numbers;
- Confirm details in writing;
- Decide on the 'message' – your charity's cause and how employees' money will make a difference;
- Make the 'ask' with Internal Champion;
- Say thank you;
- Keep in touch with employer and employees – consider involving them in your charity in voluntary roles;
- Persuade employees to increase their giving over time.

In 2012-2013, Payroll Giving raised £155 million for charities from 1,022,000 donors. Your charity should be a beneficiary of some of this!

VAT

VAT is a critical and complex area for charities. This section clarifies the issues around VAT for charity fundraising, and does not seek to address VAT rules for all aspects of charity work.

Whilst charities are subject to the same VAT rules as any other organisation, there are VAT reliefs and exemptions available specifically for registered, exempt and excepted charities, subject to certain conditions and restrictions. Charities which are not registered with the Charity Commission or which are registered in Scotland or Northern Ireland must have evidence that they are formally recognised by HMRC for tax purposes.

If your charity has an income of £79,000 or more annually, it must register for VAT. Key points are as follows:

Donations
Donations are outside the scope of VAT, provided that the donor receives nothing in return for his/her gift. VAT does not have to be accounted for on any monies received.

Fundraising events
Events organised and promoted primarily to raise money for the benefit of your charity are exempt from VAT, subject to certain conditions. The exemption covers admission fees for the event and any other income generated by the event, e.g. the sale of food or commemorative items. Only 15 fundraising events of the same kind in one financial year are VAT exempt, and the exemption does not cover the sale of surplus commemorative items after the event, nor the sale of video or audio recordings of the event in question. So-called 'charity challenge' events where participants are provided with free food and/or accommodation are also not covered by this VAT exemption.

Sponsorship
If your charity receives money, goods or services from sponsors, VAT is not payable provided that the sponsor receives no significant benefits. However, if your charity is obliged to provide the sponsor with a significant benefit in return, the sponsorship is regarded as a business activity and is taxed at the standard rate.

General areas outside fundraising where charities may pay no VAT or pay it at the reduced rate of 5% include:

- The purchase of fuel, power and water – 5%;
- Advertising – 0%;
- Purchase of certain goods for disabled people – 0%;
- The purchase of certain vehicles, e.g. ambulances and vehicles converted for people with disabilities; provided that these vehicle are purchased with charitable or donated funds – 0%;
- The purchase of medical, veterinary and scientific equipment – 0%;
- The purchase of certain rescue equipment – 0%;
- Resuscitation models for use in first aid training – 0%;
- Construction of certain buildings – e.g. hospices and village halls – 0%;
- Certain works to protected buildings. The 0% rate was removed in October 2012, but transitional arrangements for charities already engaged in alterations to protected buildings will continue until September 2015;
- Fundraising events – provided that the event is solely to raise funds for your charity and that it is a one-off, and not recurring, event – 0%.

The above list is not exhaustive, and the rules regarding VAT and charities are detailed and complex. More information can be gained from the HMRC website www.hmrc.gov.uk/charities or by calling HMRC on 0300 1234 1073.

Appendix A: SAMPLE GIFT AID CERTIFICATE

Gift Aid declaration – for past, present & future donations

Name of charity or Community Amateur Sports Club

Please treat as Gift Aid donations all qualifying gifts of money made

today ☐ in the past 4 years ☐ in the future ☐

Please tick all boxes you wish to apply.

I confirm I have paid or will pay an amount of Income Tax and/or Capital Gains Tax for each tax year (6 April to 5 April) that is at least equal to the amount of tax that all the charities or Community Amateur Sports Clubs (CASCs) that I donate to will reclaim on my gifts for that tax year. I understand that other taxes such as VAT and Council Tax do not qualify. I understand the charity will reclaim 28p of tax on every £1 that I gave up to 5 April 2008 and will reclaim 25p of tax on every £1 that I give on or after 6 April 2008.

Donor's details

Title ....First name or initial(s)...........................……

Surname ....……...

Full home address

....……

....…..

Postcode...…...…………

Date ....…...……..

Signature..…...……

Please notify the charity or CASC if you:

- Want to cancel this declaration;
- Change your name or home address;

- No longer pay sufficient tax on your income and/or capital gains.

If you pay Income Tax at the higher or additional rate and want to receive the additional tax relief due to you, you must include all your Gift Aid donations on your Self Assessment tax return or ask HM Revenue and Customs to adjust your tax code.

Appendix B: SAMPLE COVENANT

DEED OF COVENANT

I (Mr., Mrs., Miss) --
(Full Name- BLOCK CAPITALS)
of
....
....……............................
....
.................................Postcode.............................

do hereby covenant with ……. (name of charity)………that for
a period of FIVE years from the date of this Deed, or during my
lifetime, whichever is the shorter period, I will pay annually to
the said..…..(name of charity)……. such a sum as will, after de-
duction of Income Tax at the standard rate for the time being in
force, leave in the hands of ……...(name of charity)………. a
net sum of £.....................…..(figures)
....……..(words)
such sum to be paid from my general fund of taxed income, so
that I shall receive no personal or private benefit in any of the
said years from the said sum or any part thereof.

IN WITNESS WHEREOF I have set my hand
this …….(day) ……. of…….(month)……20

Signed and delivered by the said
....
(Full-Name- BLOCK CAPITALS)
SIGNATURE
....

In the presence of:
Signature of Witness
....

Occupation

....

(The witness should not be the spouse of the Covenantor)
Address

....
....
....
....
............Postcode...................

Chapter 10: Public relations

'Let's get a media campaign going – that will bring in lots of money!' is a cry I have heard many times in numerous fundraising campaigns. Alas, it is not quite that simple. Articles in the local press or radio interviews with charity leaders generate interest and create knowledge – but they rarely of themselves bring in funds.

A public relations (PR) campaign is important for successful fundraising, but it needs to be integrated with the campaign. Furthermore, successful public relations should be a means to making your fundraising campaign more successful, not an end in itself. The PR effort needs to underpin the fundraising, and this means that it needs to be targeted and timed to coincide with key milestones in the campaign.

Stage One – Preparation

The first move is to find a person – or small team – who will run the public relations for your campaign. Ideally this should be someone who is a PR professional or journalist, either current or retired. Not only will such people understand instinctively how to run your PR campaign, but they will often have the local contacts in the media which will save preparation time and make your PR more effective. If you do not have someone with PR/media experience amongst your team, see if one or more of your volunteers has a natural inclination in this area and the time to talk to journalists and PR consultants to learn the key issues in the world of PR and media communication.

PR is not, however, confined to your PR representative or team. Everyone who plays a leading role in the fundraising campaign must have a basic idea of how to communicate your charity's message. To achieve this, a short training session is advisable. Keys points for inclusion in this session are at Appendix A to this chapter.

The next move is to research your local media in depth. This doesn't simply mean local newspapers: it will include local radio and TV stations, free papers and on-line media as well as national publications specialising in your area, e.g. the *Church Times* if your campaign is for your local church and/or church hall. You need to find out the names and contact details of key personalities; deadlines for submitting newspaper copy; and the times for key news bulletins on local TV and radio. The old media adage that 'late news is no news' remains true even in the electronic age.

Stage 2 – Setting the scene

The best PR campaign in the world is unlikely to succeed unless you have the key points which will interest the media; and other personalities involved who will provide an added dimension to your campaign.

By this stage in your campaign, you will have an effective Case Statement (see Chapter 2) and probably other literature to persuade potential donors to give to your project. These will be a useful source of information which your PR person/team will be able to use – but will not be sufficient in themselves. You are not trying to convince the media to give to your campaign – unless your local paper has a 'Charity of the Year' and you would like to be it! You are trying to persuade them that your story is of public interest and will help to sell their papers, and therefore you have to convince them that a project which at first sight will only benefit a small number of people – a new school sports hall or a new roof for your church - is actually going to provide facilities for a much wider cross-section of the community, including people who are deprived, disabled or disadvantaged in other ways.

One of the ways of making your project more attractive to the media is to involve local or national celebrities who are already of media interest. You can then 'piggy-back' your project on their attractiveness to the media. We have already looked at celebrities and the 'Great & Good' as potential wealthy donors in Chapter 8. Some of those may be prepared in addition to giving to act as 'ambassadors' for your campaign, and if they are sufficiently well known they will act as a magnet for the media and thereby improve the chances of your PR campaign's success. These 'ambassadors' are usually known as Patrons or Presidents; if there are a large number, it is often the case that one person is asked to lead (Patron or President) and the remainder are designated Vice Patrons or Vice Presidents. It is vital that these people understand what is expected of them before being appointed to the role: it is difficult for anyone to act as an ambassador for a charity unless they have already given to it; and furthermore, Patrons/Presidents will be of little PR value if they are not prepared to attend fundraising events or make themselves available to the media at short notice. The bottom line is this: Patrons/Presidents must be the sort of people the public wish to read about and meet, if they are to be effective.

Stage 3 – Discussions with the media

The media are in business – to sell their airtime, newspapers etc. Many media are financed partly or largely through advertising revenues, and advertisers will only use them if they feel assured of a wide circulation/audience.

It is essential that your PR person/team visit all the local media, and at the least telephone relevant sections of the national media. This will enable you to inform the media about your charity, your project and your campaign plans; and the media to brief you on angles that interest them, deadlines and any other requirements. One charity for which I ran a fundraising campaign derived a lot of valuable publicity from a local radio

station because their leader was prepared to undertake live interviews at 0650, a time when the radio station needed live contrib-
utors but few of the latter wanted to get up and talk on the air
that early!

90% of communication with the media today is electronic,
so media releases need to be by e-mail and by using your website.

Your PR team needs to compile a handbook with contact
details of all the media and notes about what particularly interests them so that the most appropriate media can be contacted
instantly when a PR opportunity occurs.

Time spent getting to know local journalists and photogra-
phers – if possible over a drink at your expense – will not be
wasted. It will not only put names to faces, but it will enable you
to find out the flavour of their current editorial.

Do not expect the media to come to you. As well as PR
team contacts, persuade your supporters to write letters to the
press or telephone in to local radio stations – but make sure they
tell you first and, preferably, clear the contents of their letter or
what they are going to say on air with your PR team beforehand.

Stage 4 – The PR Plan

As already stated, the PR plan exists to support the fundraising
campaign. Much fundraising – trusts, national lottery, wealthy
individuals – will be unaffected by PR. However, the success of
the community fundraising campaign (see Chapter 11) will be
considerably enhanced by an effective PR campaign.

The PR plan should encompass a number of different elements. The first of these is raising the awareness of the public
about the project in general, the benefits it will bring to the community and the need for funds if it is to succeed. This is often
known as 'keeping the campaign in the public eye'. For this element of the plan to succeed, there needs to be agreement with
the media about the scope and frequency of reports, articles and
interviews so that there is a constant 'drip feed' of information
to local people about the campaign and its progress.

The second element is the underpinning of fundraising events. The community needs not only to be made aware of forthcoming events, but also to be persuaded to attend these events or to contribute at a distance, e.g. by backing campaign volunteers who are taking part in an event on behalf of the charity such as the London Marathon. For this to be effective there needs to be a build-up of TV, radio and press publicity as well as charity posters. Then, when volunteers distribute leaflets to private homes in the area, these leaflets are recognised by families who have already seen, listened to or read reports about the events, rather than being thrown into the recycling bin. This recognition will improve the chances of families attending events or supporting them financially or both. The underpinning will only be successful if the timings are worked out with local media well in advance with the result that media coverage effectively paves the way for leaflets 'drops'.

The third element is encouraging members of the general public to donate to the fundraising campaign. Some years ago, I directed a £1.5 million campaign for a local charity. We persuaded the local daily newspaper to run an article about an aspect of the charity's work and its benefit to local people about once a fortnight. We further persuaded the newspaper to carry a small voucher at the end of each article which readers could cut out, fill in and post with their donation. We raised almost £30,000 through this – not a huge sum when seen in terms of our overall target, but a sum we were very grateful to receive and which we would otherwise have had to raise elsewhere.

The final element is specific publicity for a key event – the launch of the fundraising campaign, for example, or the formal opening of a new or refurbished building. This will not only be an opportunity to register the campaign in the minds of the community, but can also be used to transmit vital messages (e.g. how much more you still need to raise) through statements by celebrities or other leading community figures which the media are likely to report 'live'. Such publicity, linked to one or more well-known figures, will not only put the project in the public's minds, but will give it credibility.

Wider PR

However good your relations with the media, your PR Campaign will need to access people who gain their information in ways other than TV, radio or the press. The following are useful methods of spreading your message, telling people about your future plans, and informing them of the successes you and your volunteers and supporters have achieved:

Newsletters
Many older people do not have access to e-mail or the web; many other people of all ages who do may not look at your website as frequently as you would wish! Therefore, consider producing a regular newsletter – no more than 4 sides of A4 – which you can send out on a monthly or quarterly basis to keep your supporters abreast of how your campaign is progressing and what you are planning next. You will also be able to tell them what you have achieved and include photos of past events in which they and their friends may have taken part.

The newsletter should ideally be sent out electronically – but you will need to give supporters the option of hard copy for the reasons stated above.

Social media
An increasing number of people – particularly young people – communicate via social media rather than e-mail or other more conventional means. Consider using Twitter to talk directly to your supporters and other stakeholders. Share insights by getting your Chairman or CMT Chairman to start a blog and connect with donors, supporters and other key figures through Facebook.

Website

In Chapter Three, we discussed the need for your CMT to have a PR representative and the steps which need to be taken to ensure that this representative is trained to promote your fundraising campaign orally, on air and in writing.

This person needs the support of an effective website. Your charity may already have one, but the chances are that it will not be fundraising-friendly.

Let us assume for a moment that your charity does not have a website. How do you go about getting one set up?

In my view, asking well-intentioned volunteers who are not professionals in website creation to do this is a mistake, however cost-effective it may seem at first sight. If you can find a volunteer who is a professional and will set up and maintain your website for nothing, that is a different matter.

There is no need to spend thousands or tens of thousands of pounds on your website. There are small but professional websites companies which will set up a very good website for £500 and maintain it for an annual fee of around 10% of this sum.

There are essentially 2 parts to an effective charity website: the first is the technical expertise and design skill of the webmaster you select; and the second is the quality of the material which goes into the site. No matter how effective your webmaster is, he/she needs high quality photos and written material from which to create a successful site for you.

Finding a cost-effective webmaster is not always easy. Fortunately, there are organisations in most areas – very often sponsored by local government – which will give you advice. They will also provide a list of webmasters in your area, although they will probably decline to recommend any specifically.

It is worth telephoning a number of the webmasters in your area, and once you have looked at their own websites and contacted other charities and organisations which use them, you should visit 3-4 webmasters and discuss your requirements, how they can meet these and at what cost. Then you will be in a position to make the best decision for your charity.

If you already have a website, should you modify this for your fundraising campaign – or set up a separate fundraising website? My view is that for most small charities, one website is sufficient. Special pages can be created for a time-limited fundraising campaign.

If you choose to have a special fundraising website, then there needs to be a clear link on both websites to the other site so that those who are interested in your charity's main activities do not find themselves unable to access this information because they are mistakenly on your fundraising campaign website – or vice versa.

Your fundraising website –or the fundraising pages of your existing website – should have the following as a minimum:

•   A prominent 'DONATE' button on every page, not just on the fundraising page(s);

•   A page/pages describing the aims of the fundraising campaign, project(s) and campaign costs/target;

•   A 'News' page which should include past and future events (with reports for the former). This will require regular (i.e. at least weekly) updating;

•   A page listing different giving options (including text giving) and how these may be accessed;

•   Details of how would-be supporters can help your campaign in other ways – voluntary tasks in the Campaign Office, organising fundraising events, donating gifts-in-kind;

•   A contact page to enable donors and other supporters to reach your Campaign Office. It is worth remembering g that many older people do not have e-mail, so a postal address and fax number should be included.

If the cost of setting up a professional website is beyond your charity's resources, consider iT4 Communities, set up in 2002 as a charitable programme of the Worshipful Company of Information Technologists, one of the London City Livery Companies. In its first 7 years of operation, the programme helped 2,500 charities by putting them in touch with professionals for the free provision of IT-related projects, such as building websites or databases.

An *aide mémoire* for setting up fundraising web pages is at Appendix B to this chapter.

Checklist

Preparation
- PR representative or team selected;
- If not professional, opportunity for him/her/them to meet PR/media professionals;
- PR training organised for key volunteers;
- Research local media – newspapers? Radio? TV? Online?
- Research relevant national media;
- Create lists of media and representatives' contact details;
- Understand deadlines and other key requirements.

Setting the scene
- Persuasive case for media support;
- Community value of your project;
- Patrons or Presidents researched and appointed.

Discussions with media
- Visit local media;
- Discuss your project and their deadlines/interests;
- Meet journalists and discuss your campaign with them;
- Persuade supporters to write to the local press or call in to local radio stations;

• Create an aide mémoire for all local and relevant national media with names, telephone numbers, e-mail addresses.

PR Plan

• Raising public awareness;
• Underpinning fundraising events;
• Encouraging the public to give;
• List of key events and specific publicity required;
• Does plan support fundraising campaign.

Appendix A: PUBLIC RELATIONS TRAINING

Your Campaign will need at least one person who is an able public speaker and a fluent writer and who can communicate your key messages effectively, both orally and in writing.

However, everyone in your campaign needs to be 'on-message', and this can best be achieved by a basic training session.

Public speaking
- Know your subject. If talking about the fundraising campaign, you will need to have at your fingertips the key facts about it: what are you trying to raise money for? How much money are you trying to raise? Why is this campaign necessary? A thorough knowledge of the campaign will enhance your credibility and will make it more likely that others will give their support;
- Know your audience. Concentrate on those aspects of your campaign which are most likely to interest your audience. Imagine you are raising funds for a new village or community hall. The Board of Directors of a local company will be interested in the conference and hospitality facilities you intend creating; whereas the parents, staff and governors of the nearby primary schools will be interested in after-school and holiday activities and any indoor or outdoor sports which will be on offer;
- Don't bluff. If you don't know the answer to a question, say so – but promise that you will find out and revert to the enquirer;
- Ask for donations. Even if you are being interviewed by the local radio station about the new facilities your fundraising campaign will create, get in a request for funding and tell your audience where to send their donations;
- Live or recorded? If you have the choice of either a live or recorded TV or radio interview, consider the pros and cons. A live interview ensures that whatever you want to say reaches your audience, whereas a radio or TV station can edit

167

out bits of a recorded interview. On the other hand, a slip-up or mistake on a recorded interview can be corrected and the interview re-recorded – a luxury which does not exist when you are 'live'!

Writing

• Whilst good public speaking is important, you will also need to get the campaign message across in writing, particularly when dealing with the press;

• Contrary to popular belief, the press rarely 'misquote' what members of the public say or write, but they do emphasise the points which they believe will sell their newspapers and magazines;

• Journalists are busy people and they have an editor to please. So make it easy for them! If you can take and supply good quality photos for them to use, do so as it will save them sending a photographer to your event;

• Write an article or report which will need no or little editing. If you read professional newspaper reports, especially in the tabloid press, you will note that the key messages are in the early paragraphs with the less essential information lower down. This is because editors cut from the bottom up. So don't leave important information – like how and where to send donations – to the end of your piece.

Appendix B: WEBSITE FUNDRAISING PAGES AIDE MÉMOIRE

Irrespective of whether you are creating a new website for your fundraising campaign or modifying an existing one, the following should be borne in mind. The whole aim of the website from your campaign standpoint is to persuade people to give and to continue giving. You should therefore have pages which:

• Explain to potential donors what the options are – bank transfer; cheque; CAF voucher; credit/debit card; on-line; text – but also how they should best access these options and what advantages there are in specific options, both for them and for your charity;

• Explain the options for regular as well as one-off donations – standing orders; direct debits; covenants;

• Outline other gift options such as transfers of shares or donations of property;

• Ask them whether they wish to be regularly contacted by your charity and, if so, how often and by what means;

• Ask them whether they would like to be involved as a volunteer with your charity either during your specific fundraising campaign or on a regular basis;

• Ask them if they would like any specific information or literature regarding your campaign;

• Offer them a range of means for contacting the Campaign office including telephone and fax numbers; e-mail address; and postal address. An e-mail response via a page with drop-down boxes will make contact easier for potential donors and supporters.

In addition to the above, it is wise to have a news page or pages which will not only inform people of past successes but also provide a calendar of future events in which they may wish to take part.

The news pages also offer the opportunity to thank donors when specific aspects of the project are complete or phased targets within the campaign are achieved. Saying 'Thank You' is the most important part of any charity-donor relationship – and thanks cannot be repeated too often both privately (via letter) and in public on your website (unless of course a donor has particularly asked to remain anonymous).

Finally, ensure there is a 'DONATE' logo on each page of the website in a clearly visible place. You cannot afford to lose donors because they get bored with trying to find the specific donations page(s).

Chapter 11: Community fundraising

Community fundraising is the most popular aspect of fundraising amongst volunteers. It is popular for 2 principal reasons:
- Most volunteers enjoy organising an event – either one-off or continuing – and because they enjoy organising events, they convince themselves that events raise lots of money!
- It avoids them having to ask others for gifts.

Community fundraising should take place towards the end of your fundraising campaign, when all other sources of funding have been exhausted. The reasons for this are:
- Tackling the best sources of funds early on will sustain a positive, successful view of the campaign right from the start – both amongst your volunteers and in the community at large;
- The Campaign should start with asking your immediate supporters for gifts, together with organisations which exist to donate funds to charities and other selected organisations, e.g. grant-making trusts and the National Lottery. This will not only build up your funds but will show to those more peripherally involved that the charity's key supporters and major funding organisations are totally committed to the campaign;
- Donors early in the campaign will be happy later on to buy raffle tickets, tickets for a dinner or reception or support athletes in an event. They will have, in effect, given twice – on the second occasion they will not perceive their act as giving, because they may receive a 'reward' for their expenditure. However, if the events take place in the early stages of a campaign, many people will buy a raffle ticket and then refer to this as their 'donation'. This is called 'inoculation' in

fundraising, and effectively permits donors to give much less than they would have done had they been asked face-to-face by the right person.

The exception to the above is raising funds through recycling schemes. This can be started early on, and will serve to involve more people (especially those of school age) in the campaign and raise its profile.

Organisation

Unless your Campaign Management Team is large and its members have plenty of time to devote to the campaign, you will need to set up a Community Fundraising Team (CFT) to organise the community fundraising. This should be led by a volunteer with excellent personal community contacts, and need consist of no more than 4-6 people.

The important point is that the CFT is there to organise the community fundraising programme, not to organise individual events. It will therefore need to meet before the community fundraising programme is launched and decide on the following:

- How often events should take place? (Probably no more than one a month);
- Who should be asked to organise events: individual supporters; organisations in the community outside the charity itself. Groups who might be enlisted to run events include churches; schools; business organisations such as Rotary, Lions and Round Table; and other community organisations such as the Women's Institute or the Royal British Legion;
- What sort of events should be organised – even if the CFT decide to leave this decision to those organising individual events, the latter will probably want suggestions from the CFT. In addition, the CFT should give advice so that events have the best chances of success, e.g. that clashes with sports and other local and national occasions are avoided and

that appropriate permissions are sought where necessary from local Councils, the Police and other bodies.

Throughout the community fundraising campaign, the CFT will need to keep a close watch on the events programme and those organising events. The CFT will also need to liaise closely with the PR volunteer/team to ensure that each event receives timely publicity appropriate to the activities involved.

Events

Events can and do raise substantial sums for charity – but more often than not they fail to do this. So as to avoid financial disaster, the CFT should encourage event organisers to note the following:

•   All costs for an event should be sponsored, so that even if only £5 worth of raffle tickets are sold, that represents £5 net income for the fundraising campaign;

•   If the event is a ticket entry affair, informal discussions should be held with the sponsors to agree a minimum number of attenders for the event to be deemed a success, together with a decision date on which the event is cancelled or postponed should the number fail to reach the minimum set;

•   If the event is an outdoor one and entry tickets are being sold, it is important that only those who buy tickets can benefit. This is particularly difficult to achieve if the event is not in a stadium or visually restricted area and can be watched from a distance, such as a flying display or balloon festival;

•   Events are normally most successful if run at the weekends, in the evenings or on Bank Holidays. The problem with this is that everyone knows this, so that on these occasions there are likely to be competing events, especially in the summer months, and even at local level. Therefore the choice of date and the importance of close liaison with the campaign's

PR team loom very large if the event is to draw the crowds
necessary for its success;

• Events such as marathons or even lesser road runs need
local council permission and probably will require public
roads to be closed to traffic. On top of this, organisers will
need to provide First Aid crews, changing areas and possibly
showers, refreshments and a variety of other support facilities – as well as volunteers to act as start/finish staff, mar-
shals etc. All this means that such events cannot be organised
overnight, but will need months of careful and detailed planning and negotiation;

• Do not forget insurance. We live in a litigious world,
and although most people will think twice about suing a charity if, for example, they sustain an injury running a half marathon or their clothes are ruined when their dragon boat
capsizes, you need to have a plan for when events go wrong.
This plan should be drawn up well in advance by the CMT
in close cooperation with the PR team and event organisers.
In this way, minimum damage – both financial and reputa-
tional – will be suffered if there is an accident.

Sales

Most people have items which are saleable in their attics, garages
and sheds. Many more have items in those places which are not
saleable! The days of holding jumble sales to raise serious money
are over; the need now is to concentrate on specific market seg-
ments and to make buying as easy for the potential purchaser as
it is in a shop or supermarket.

Children's clothes and some toys make good money for
charity. Make sure that the sale organisers borrow mobile hanging rails if possible, or folding tables if hangers are unavailable.
Clothes should be clean, in good condition and priced. They
should also be arranged by size/age range, sex and type (i.e rain-
coats not mixed in with party frocks), so that prospective purchasers can see at a glance whether there is anything they want

in the size they are seeking. Pricing should be researched and realistic: too high and the items will not sell; too low and the maximum value for your campaign will not have been realised. There are few occasions these days when an 'Everything at 50p' notice is appropriate!

Bric-à-brac sales are past their sell-by date today. No one wants your odd teacups or mismatched 1980s cutlery unless they are students – so if you are nowhere near a university or FE college, forget these. However, people do have items of value stashed away that they are prepared to give to charity – and many local jewellers will value these before the sale free of charge as a contribution to your campaign.

Books and DVDs can raise money – but again, it is best to research these and notify booksellers or known enthusiasts so that you generate maximum interest, having also researched the value of items via on-line sources.

Home produce – cakes, jams, honey, even fresh garden vegetables – are still as popular as ever. You should aim to undercut local supermarkets with your offerings – but not by too much. Many years ago my garden produced an annual surplus of cooking apples. The first year I tried giving them away – but without success. In later years I offered them for sale at 50% of the local supermarket price with proceeds going to the village church. They went in no time at all!

Community activities

The Scouts' 'Bob-a-Job' used to be a popular way of fundraising in the 20th Century. Every Easter holidays, Scouts would jump on their bicycles and go round their neighbourhoods offering to wash cars, dig gardens and other activities for 1/- (or often a bit more). Today this type of activity tends to be undertaken by groups in aid of charity.

Examples of activities which benefit the wider community and for which charges can be made include:

- Car washing;

- Gardening;
- Packing carrier bags with groceries;
- Dog walking;
- Litter picking.

The legal aspects need close consideration in terms of where these activities can be carried out; the extent to which children can take part with or without adult supervision; and the permissions which have to be sought and the timeframe for these.

Street collections

This age-old method of collecting for charity has endured some bad press in recent years, largely as the result of some charities employing people to seek donations and paying them according to their results. This so-called 'chugging' (= 'charity mugging') and its publicity should not put you off using volunteers to shake tins outside your local railway station or supermarket.

Remember that open buckets are no longer legal and that you will need to buy special collecting tins (actually, they are usually plastic these days) together with tamper-proof seals which prevent the collectors opening them and removing donations.

Collectors now need photo ID and you will need permission of the local council as well as that of the railway company or supermarket before you can start collecting.

Finally – don't forget to make arrangements to store safely and pay in the monies collected at the end of the collecting day (which will probably be after the banks have closed).

Lotteries and Raffles

A Lottery is a game where people can buy tickets with a chance of winning a prize; and a raffle is a form of lottery. There must be at least one prize, and winning a prize must be dependent only on chance. If you are considering a lottery (including a raffle) in support of your campaign, the first step you need to take is to determine whether you need a licence or not.

You first port of all is your local District or Borough Council. They will advise you what permission you need if any and whether you will need a licence from the Gambling Commission.

Essentially, if you wish to sell tickets to the general public over an extended period of time, you will need a licence from the Gambling Commission. However, there are certain types of lottery which are 'exempt':

• Small society lotteries. These must be promoted for the benefit of a non-commercial society, and the value of the tickets on sale must be £20,000 or less and the annual proceeds £250,000 or less. These lotteries must still be registered with your District or Borough Council;

• Incidental, non-commercial lotteries. These are typically lotteries held at fundraising events. They must not be for private gain; tickets must only be sold at the event, where the draw must also take place; prizes – whether donated or bought – cannot total more than £500; and no more than £100 can be deducted from sales for costs;

• Private lotteries. There are several different types of private lottery. Two of the most common are Work Lotteries and Residents' Lotteries: they must be organised on a single site or premises; they must not be run for profit; and all the proceeds must be used for prizes or reasonable expenses in organising the lottery. A Private Society Lottery can be used for fundraising: the Lottery can be promoted on the organisation's premises with written authorisation from the organisation; tickets are sold to the organisation's staff and members on the premises; and the tickets must give the name and address of the promoters, the ticket price and state who can buy the tickets;

• Customer lotteries. These may be run by occupiers of a business premises. Tickets can only be sold to customers on a single premises, and the total value of the prize must not exceed £50. No profit can be made from the Lottery.

Irrespective of whether a licence is needed or not, all tickets must be sold for the same price (e.g. you cannot sell 10 for the price of 8) – except in the case of incidental, non-commercial lotteries.

Auctions

Auctions are often held at one-off fundraising events such as dinners and receptions. They can be an effective way of raising funds for your campaign, especially if you can persuade a professional auctioneer to give his/her services for nothing. Auctions also have the advantage of not falling under gambling law.

However, auctions are still subject to consumer legislation, including the Trades Descriptions Act 1968. It is also important to establish terms and conditions and consider potential reserve prices – and agree these with the auctioneer in advance of the auction.

Recycling

Recycling is on the increase – but not everyone is aware that some of this can benefit charities. Schemes worth considering include:

- Textiles which are too worn to be resold. These include leather items such as belts and shoes, trainers and rubber boots. There are a number of companies offering this service for charity, so there is no need to place these items in your local supermarket 'bank'. Some companies will collect bins liners full of textiles – but they will give less to your charity than if you take your bin liners to a central collection point. Bear in mind that recycling companies will pay your charity on the weight of the bags – so encourage supporters to put in their old boots and shoes as well as worn-out drying-up cloths!

• Mobile 'phones, ink and toner cartridges. This is potentially a very good fundraising area if you can persuade local companies to donate these items after they have donated to your campaign or set up a Payroll Giving Scheme. But be aware that different companies on-line have different rules and pay varying amounts. Some offer only a few pence for perfectly serviceable mobiles which they will then sell overseas for many pounds. The best companies taking printer ink and toner cartridges will send you collection boxes which they will then collect free of charge; pay you for the cartridges which have value; and dispose of those which do not at no cost to you. The worst will charge for the disposal of nil value cartridges and deduct this cost from the meagre amounts they pay for those than can be recycled. You have been warned!

• Cars. A relative newcomer to the charity recycling world is Giveacar. Launched in January 2010, within 2 years it had raised £500,000 for charities, including £85,000 for Cancer Research UK alone. If your car is a MoT failure or otherwise due for scrapping, you can call Giveacar who will collect it from you at no charge. They will then assess the car's scrap value, and give this sum to a charity of your choice. If your car is roadworthy and has a current MoT certificate, Giveacar will collect the car and send it to auction. You can then decide whether 100% of the proceeds (less seller's premium) go to the charity of your choice, or whether the proceeds are split 50-50 between you and the charity. However, your charity needs to register with Giveacar before you can be chosen by a donor as the recipient of their car's sale price or scrap value. Their contact details are www.giveacar.co.uk or 020 0011 1664;

• Other commodities such as books, furniture – indeed almost anything which might otherwise be offloaded at a council recycling site or put in the weekly rubbish/recycling collection.

On-line

There are a number of search engines which give part of their revenues to charity, and this is a painless way for all your charity's supporters to raise funds for your campaign. To start the process:

- Your charity will need to register with its chosen search engine(s);
- Supporters and members of the community then need to be persuaded to use that search engine whenever they surf the net or make a transaction on-line, and to nominate your charity as the recipient of each search engine donation.

Funds are then generated in 2 ways:

- Every time a supporter clicks on an advertiser using the agreed search engine, your charity receives a small donation;
- If your charity can persuade advertisers on the search engine's site to be its sponsor, you will receive a percentage of the sponsorship revenues.

A number of search engines offer this service to charity including Google, Yahoo!, Live Search and Every Click.

More recently, BT and Vodafone have set up on-line and text donation schemes. Vodafone's JustGiving was the first on-line, followed by BT's Mydonate. Initially, JustGiving made a charge while Mydonate was free, but in 2011 Vodafone extended their scheme to allow UK donors to give money to charity free of charge by text message. These have been joined by Virgin Money Giving and Bmycharity.

This system of giving is particularly popular with younger donors, and it is well worthwhile your charity considering one of these websites. Virgin Money Giving provides a useful chart on its website, comparing the services it provides with those of JustGiving and Bmycharity.

Birthday, Christmas, wedding presents and funeral donations

Many people, especially the aged, feel that they no longer want gifts for their birthdays or at Christmas when postage and packing can add significantly to the donor's overall costs. An alternative option is to offer to make a gift to a charity of the recipient's choice of the same size as the donor would have spent on a present. This not only eliminates postage and packing costs, but it allows those who have all the material goods they need to contribute to worthy causes at no cost to themselves.

Many wedding couples also choose to have some or all of their wedding presents in the form of donations to charities they choose. It has also long been a practice to ask for donations to be given to a charity in lieu of funeral flowers. However, in practice few of the deceased think about this and express a clear wish before they die. As a result, relatives and friends are left wondering which charity the deceased might have wished them to support. A sensible move is to brief local funeral directors on your fundraising campaign, so that they can tactfully suggest to unsure relatives that they should consider donations to your charity and its campaign.

Challenge events

A number of companies have set up what are called 'challenge' events as a means of raising funds for charities. The principal idea behind this follows on from long-established competitions like the London Marathon, and the basis is that charity volunteers should enjoy themselves undertaking physical – and sometimes mentally – challenging activities in the UK or overseas.

This can be a very successful way for people – especially young people – to raise money for your charity. However, you

181

should be aware that challenge events are not free and participants will be expected to pay often substantial travel and training costs – and then fundraise on top of these.

Crowdfunding

What is Crowdfunding?
Originating in the United States, it is a concept where websites are set up which allow organisations or people to raise money for a project online through multiple donations or loans made by a number of donors over a short space of time. Crowdfunding was used to fund Barack Obama's 2008 presidential campaign.

In the UK the best known website for Crowdfunding is Peoplefund.it, founded in late 2011. The Bicycle Academy raised £140,000 through Peoplefund.it in just 6 days, but there have been some unsuccessful examples too. One reason for this is that some charities have failed to realise that Crowdfunding complements more conventional fundraising and needs a strategy, a plan and a network to succeed.

Crowdfunding is worth considering – but make sure that you have done your homework and taken advice about the likely attractiveness of your charity and its project to an audience beyond your local area.

There are of course numerous other ways of raising funds through community fundraising, and a number of books have been written on ways of achieving this, e.g. *250+ fundraising ideas for your charity, society, school and PTA* by Paige Robinson.

Checklist

Organisation
- Community Fundraising Team (CFT) recruited;
- CFT Chairman appointed;

- CFT met and decided on community fundraising programme;
- CFT liaised with PR team.

Events
- Event organisers sought and briefed;
- Dates for events agreed with organisers;
- Checked that events are sponsored or costs otherwise covered;
- Checked that all local council and other permissions sought and obtained;
- Events publicised;
- Contingency plan for accidents and other problems produced and discussed with PR;
- Events insurance policy(ies) taken out.

Sales
- Types of sales agreed with organisers;
- Organisers sought professional advice on value of sales items where appropriate;
- Goods attractively laid out and clothing sized;
- All items realistically priced;
- Sales publicised.

Community activities
- Activities planned by organisers;
- Participants sought and signed up;
- Local council and other permissions sought;
- Role of children/young people clarified;
- Activities publicised.

Street collections
- Equipment obtained – collection boxes, photo IDs;
- Local council and other permissions sought;
- Collectors briefed on legal aspects;
- Arrangements for keeping/paying in cash after collection day has ended;
- Collections and areas publicised.

Lotteries and raffles
- Advice sought from District or Borough Council;
- Is Lottery exempt?
- Category of lottery/raffle determined;
- Permission/Licence obtained;
- Other regulations relevant to the chosen category complied with.

Auction
- Event and location determined;
- Auctioneer's services agreed;
- Consumer legislation provisions met;
- Terms and conditions agreed;
- Reserve prices agreed with auctioneer.

Recycling
- Textile collections organised;
- Storage for textile bags/bin liners;
- Set up arrangements with textile recycling company;
- Mobile 'phone, printer ink and toner recycling organised;
- Asked local companies, schools, local councils to donate their cartridges;
- Checked which recycling companies offer best deal;
- Storage for 'phones and cartridges organised;
- Considered Giveacar scheme;
- Publicised recycling programmes;
- Any other items which can be recycling for cash.

On-line
- Search engines checked and compared;
- Charity registered with chosen search engine(s);
- Supporters and local community informed and reminded;
- Registered with JustGiving or Mydonate.

Charity donations in lieu of presents/funeral flowers
- Supporters briefed and informed;
- Community encouraged to participate;
- Forthcoming weddings in the local press checked by volunteers and approaches made;
- Funeral directors informed and briefed on your fundraising campaign and its community benefits.

Chapter 12: Support material

However small your charity and irrespective of the level of funding your campaign needs, you will need visual material to back it up. A survey once showed that 85% of what we take in is from visual sources – though avid radio listeners might not agree!

The advantages of the written word over the spoken word are:

• The spoken word can easily be forgotten, whereas the written word can be referred to over and over again;

• Receptiveness to the spoken word will depend on the listener(s) – effective if they are alert, enthusiastic and concentrating on the speaker but ineffective if they are tired, disinterested or other matters divert their attention. In contrast, the written word can be put on one side by a recipient until he/she is in the frame of mind to absorb it.

Your campaign will already have produced a Case Statement (see Chapter Two) and this is the baseline document on which future support material will be created.

Not every campaign will require a full range of support material – but each campaign will need some form of hardcopy which can be distributed to supporters and potential donors.

Brochures and leaflets

The traditional brochures and leaflets still play an important part in most fundraising campaigns, since costs at the lower end of the market allow even small charities to distribute or mail drop so that each person in, say, a large country village receives his or her own copy. The main types of literature are as follows:

Campaign leaflets

These are usually in A4 tri-fold and provide you with 6 panels (3 on either side of the paper). This fits easily through a letterbox or in a DL envelope.

In addition, printers have a special size not readily available in stationery shops which adds an extra fold and therefore 2 more panels to the leaflet. This can be helpful if your charity either has a complex message to communicate or a particular number of high profile supporters whose photographs and/or quotes you wish to include.

Leaflets can be glossy, multi-coloured and printed; or matt, single or 2 colour and produced on a reasonable photocopier. The decision as to which type is adopted will be based partly on your charity finances and partly on the impression you wish to create with potential donors. On the one hand, a printed glossy leaflet could be off-putting in that it could suggest that your charity has money to spare and therefore does not really need further gifts. On the other hand, a photocopied leaflet can create an impression of a campaign which is not professionally organised and/or is not serious about what it wishes to achieve.

Campaign leaflets should include a brief summary of your charity's aims and activities; a résumé of the campaign – how much it seeks to raise, why, and what the campaign's elements or projects are; photographs and/or drawings where appropriate; details of high profile Patron/Vice Patrons or President/Vice Presidents; quotes from key figures in the campaign; contact details for the campaign office; and a detachable form with giving options and return address.

Consideration should be given to offering potential donors and supporters a freepost return address. Royal Mail charges a one-off fee (currently £86) for this service, and then a fee per letter delivered, which can be set at either 1st or 2nd class rate. On top of this your charity may choose to have freepost envelopes printed: there are a number of different styles approved by Royal Mail from which you can choose.

Campaign brochures

A campaign brochure is an altogether more comprehensive publication than a campaign leaflet. Professionally printed, it will be in stiff card, multicolour and high visibility. It is usually in A4 portrait or landscape, but can be in A5 if the particular situation demands a smaller document.

It will contain full details about the charity; the project for which funds are being raised; and all the different ways of giving tax-efficiently.

The campaign brochure will include a comprehensive selection of relevant photographs and, in the case of a building or building refurbishment project, architects' plans and an artist's impression of how the new or refurbished building will appear when complete.

Frequently the campaign brochure will feature a pocket in the back cover into which gift aid forms, covenant forms and update information or information relevant to specific donors can be inserted.

Costs of a campaign brochure will run into four-figure sums and upwards. Campaign brochures are therefore only appropriate where the fundraising campaign is geographically wide-ranging, or where there are a number of likely major individual and/or corporate donors for whom a simple campaign leaflet would be inappropriate.

Special Prospects Documents

Special Prospects Documents (SPD) – or Advance Information Documents as they are sometimes known – are appropriate if your Campaign Management Team and subsequent evaluation of donors have identified key individual or corporate donors which the CMT wishes to bring on board early in the campaign. This might be particularly important if research indicates that your campaign project(s) are unlikely to create a high degree of credibility and/or support in the community, and that the campaign will therefore need an early boost if it is to achieve its target.

SPDs need to be more comprehensive in the information they provide than can be achieved in a campaign leaflet, but their style and cost needs to be much more modest than those of a campaign brochure. The reason for this is that major donors at the start of a challenging campaign have to be convinced that the charity really does need their financial support with leading gifts which will convince others to donate.

The SPD should have all the technical details and the giving options that would appear in a campaign brochure, together with a costed list of specific items or elements of the projects for those who would wish to fund one particular aspect of the campaign.

The SPD should be photocopied and then bound using comb or ring binding with stiff front and back covers. These types of bindings serve a dual purpose: first, their style emphasises cost-effectiveness and the need for donors' support; and secondly, the form of binding allows them to be updated as the campaign progresses without the need to reprint the whole document.

Consideration should also be given to including a script for face-to-face 'asks' if it is clear from the training sessions (see p.133) that a number of volunteers with good contacts are likely to find a successful 'ask' difficult to achieve based on the information contained in the SPD alone.

DVDs

DVDs are becoming increasingly popular as a method of raising support for fundraising campaigns. They have the advantage of enabling key members and supporters of your charity and its fundraising campaign to communicate their messages against a backdrop of the campaign project(s). They are also very useful for briefing large audiences in situations where it may be difficult to assemble the necessary speakers in person.

The cost of producing and distributing a professional DVD will probably be as much as much as those of an A4 campaign facilities now available; thanking them for their help and support during the campaign; and urging them to use, and encourage others to use, the facilities now available;

• Records need to be archived and arrangements made to update them at least twice a year. This seemingly onerous task should only need half a day per update and will save your charity time, money and hassle when you come to the next campaign.

Before the Campaign Office closes, consideration should be given to mounting a short legacy campaign to encourage your enthusiastic donors and supporters to remember your charity in their Will. There is no better time than this for a legacy campaign: everyone will be on the crest of a wave, delighted that their donations and hard work have achieved the aim, and feeling a warm glow towards your charity.

You can 'sell' the legacy campaign on the grounds of sustainability and you will be able to say that you are not asking for more money now, just a bequest which will enable future generations to continue enjoying what they have helped achieve.

Some notes on running a low-key legacy campaign at the end of your fundraising campaign are at Appendix A to this chapter.

Then – you can relax, until the next campaign!

Checklist

Finale Event
• Location;
• Midday, afternoon or evening;
• What sort of refreshments?
• Sponsorship for this, or out of campaign funds;
• Keynote speech;
• Guest list;
• PR informed media;

- Information hand-out/media release detailing new facilities;
- CMT Chairman to thank donors/supporters.

Closing Campaign Office

- All likely/expected donations received, accounted for and thanked for;
- Thank you letters to 'home team', signed by Charity Chairman or Chairman of CMT;
- Letters to local authorities, community groups and media detailing new/improved community facilities now available;
- Records archived and arrangements made for updating them;
- Consideration given to mounting short legacy campaign.

brochure and, unlike a SPD, they cannot easily be changed once produced. There is also a danger that they may be ignored by part of their target audience, as sitting down to watch a DVD requires a greater effort than leafing through a campaign brochure!

Souvenirs

Campaign Management Teams traditionally like to invest in special biros, mugs, t-shirts and other items which promote fundraising campaigns and at the same time create an income stream.

Unfortunately, the theory behind this is rarely borne out in the reality. There are a number of reasons for this:

- First, a proportion of souvenirs which are supposed to be sold in aid of the campaign are often given to campaign volunteers and others as free gifts. This means that the items actually sold not only have to return a profit on their purchase price, but also have to cover the purchase price and loss of profit on the items given away;
- Secondly, many allegedly 'attractive' items fail to sell, or sell in sufficient quantity. For example, whilst many adults think that having their children in their local hospice or church campaign T-shirt is great, the children and young people themselves do not find this idea at all 'cool'. The result: piles of unsold children's T-shirts!
- Thirdly, the potentially really attractive souvenirs – those which are unique to your campaign – are probably prohibitively expensive to produce, especially in small numbers. The souvenirs which are cheap to have 'personalised' for your campaign will be almost identical to ones being sold by other charities up and down the country.

My rule for souvenirs is this: obtain samples from suppliers and put on a display for your volunteers and supporters, with costs and personalisation options. Request orders with cash up front by a published date, and then order only those souvenirs for which you have been paid. This guarantees a certain profit level and avoids unsold items. Once the initial orders have been delivered, further orders may be received as other supporters see what they have missed. These too should be supplied on the basis of people paying for their order before the order is submitted to the supplier.

Checklist

Brochures and leaflets
- CMT chosen which form(s) of literature campaign requires;
- Drafted and decided format, size, print quality and content;
- Decided on quantity to be produced;
- Decided on donor reply system including Freepost.

DVDs
- Is a DVD appropriate?
- Quotes from different production companies;
- Occasions for use.

Souvenirs
- Are these necessary/ is there a demand?
- Researched suppliers and ordered samples;
- CMT and key volunteers assessed saleability;
- Policy on free gifts;
- Orders sought and payment taken;
- Demand for repeat orders.

Chapter 13: And finally ...

Your campaign has come to a successful conclusion and you have achieved or exceeded your campaign target. Congratulations!!

So that's it?

Well, not quite.

Remember the problems you faced setting up a fundraising campaign from scratch because your charity had never run a campaign before or, if they had, failed to keep records? Now is your opportunity to build on what you have achieved and so provide sustainability for your charity in the future.

Finale Event

First, though, you will want to celebrate your success. So start with a Finale Event. This event has a number of aims:

- Tell the whole community what you have achieved;
- Thank them – and your volunteers and supporters – for the work they have put in, the funds they have given or raised, the events they have organised;
- Explain when your new or refurbished facilities, building or equipment will be available for community use;
- Highlight the improvements that the fundraising campaign has brought – especially to disadvantaged groups and people with physical or learning disabilities.

Ideally, this event should be:

- A reception or buffet at your charity's headquarters or, if appropriate, at the newly built or refurbished facilities;
- An occasion to mark the point at which your new or refurbished facilities or other project(s) become available for public use;

• An opportunity for your Patron or President to make a keynote speech which your PR team will ensure gets maximum local media coverage.

You will need to decide who is to be invited (often a difficult minefield to navigate!):
• The general public?
• Your volunteers, donors, Patron/Vice Patrons or President/Vice Presidents, local celebrities including the 'Great & Good', local politicians and other movers and shakers?
• Just those who have contributed to the campaign – by gifts, voluntary work or organising events?

It is important not to offend people by failing to ask them; but it is equally important not to have an expensive event for everyone so that questions are asked about the source of the funds for this.

Unless you can arrange for the Finale Event to be sponsored, my advice is to ask everyone who has had some involvement, even if that involvement has not been very much. Keep costs low by making the refreshments simple if a large number of guests are attending.

Closing the Campaign Office

The Campaign Office will need to stay open for about 3 months after your campaign ends. The reasons for this are:
• Donations will gradually tail off once it is known that your campaign has been successfully concluded. They won't just stop overnight;
• Individual thank-you letters, signed by your Charity Chairman or CMT Chairman, will need to be produced to all key volunteers for his/her signature;
• Letters to local authorities, community groups and the media should be written, telling them about the wonderful

facilities now available; thanking them for their help and support during the campaign; and urging them to use, and encourage others to use, the facilities now available;

• Records need to be archived and arrangements made to update them at least twice a year. This seemingly onerous task should only need half a day per update and will save your charity time, money and hassle when you come to the next campaign.

Before the Campaign Office closes, consideration should be given to mounting a short legacy campaign to encourage your enthusiastic donors and supporters to remember your charity in their Will. There is no better time than this for a legacy campaign: everyone will be on the crest of a wave, delighted that their donations and hard work have achieved the aim, and feeling a warm glow towards your charity.

You can 'sell' the legacy campaign on the grounds of sustainability and you will be able to say that you are not asking for more money now, just a bequest which will enable future generations to continue enjoying what they have helped achieve.

Some notes on running a low-key legacy campaign at the end of your fundraising campaign are at Appendix A to this chapter.

Then – you can relax, until the next campaign!

Checklist

Finale Event
- Location;
- Midday, afternoon or evening;
- What sort of refreshments?
- Sponsorship for this, or out of campaign funds;
- Keynote speech;
- Guest list;
- PR informed media;

- Information hand-out/media release detailing new facilities;
- CMT Chairman to thank donors/supporters.

Closing Campaign Office

- All likely/expected donations received, accounted for and thanked for;
- Thank you letters to 'home team', signed by Charity Chairman or Chairman of CMT;
- Letters to local authorities, community groups and media detailing new/improved community facilities now available;
- Records archived and arrangements made for updating them;
- Consideration given to mounting short legacy campaign.

Appendix A: LEGACY CAMPAIGNS – KEY POINTS

A legacy is the only way that you can give without it costing you anything! More and more people today are worrying about their cost of living in old age, so are unwilling to give much to charity during their lifetime. A legacy is therefore an ideal giving vehicle for our aging population.

The Steps
Donors need to have a Will. If they do, a legacy can be added to it. If they do not, your charity may like to set up an informal arrangement with a local solicitor whereby the firm of solicitors provides a free Will service on the understanding (not guaranteed!) that those taking advantage of this make a legacy to your charity.

Donors need to decide what type of legacy they are going to make: a Specific Legacy, that is to say a defined asset such as a house, car or piece of jewelry. If the asset cannot be found on the death of the donor, the legacy 'fails'. A Pecuniary Legacy, that is a specific cash sum. A Residual Legacy, that is a share of the entirety of what remains of their estate once other gifts, debts, expenses and taxes have been paid.

Your charity should try to persuade donors where possible to make a Residual Legacy rather than a Pecuniary one, as the value of the latter is likely to fall the longer the donor lives.

Your charity needs to decide whom it is going to target – probably the donors and supporters of the recently completed fundraising campaign; but possibly also others if volunteers know of aged people supportive of your charity but unable or unwilling to give during their lifetime. Statistics show the donors from your fundraising campaign and your committed volunteers are more likely to make a legacy than others who support or show interest in your charity.

A letter should be produced and signed by the CMT Chairman, stating the reasons for the legacy request so soon after a successful fundraising campaign. Ensure you include suggested wording for their Will and a suggested codicil form, and enclose a response mechanism. The latter should be optional and this should be made clear: people are more likely to respond if you tell them they do not need to do so!

Consider follow-up by telephone or other means – but have a clear plan of what you want the legacy campaign to achieve before investing time and resources in it.

A legacy campaign is inappropriate for a capital fundraising campaign which seeks to raise a specific sum within a defined timeframe. However, it is ideal if an endowment fund is needed to ensure that what has been achieved in the fundraising campaign is effectively sustained for the future.

This Appendix does not provide an *aide mémoire* for a major stand-alone legacy campaign. However, it does provide the main points to be covered in a low-key campaign to provide sustainability following a successful fundraising campaign.

References

Professional bodies

Arts Councils
There are 4 Arts Councils in the UK: Arts Council England; the Scottish Arts Council; Arts Council of Wales; and the Arts Council of Northern Ireland. These government-funded bodies are dedicated to promoting performing, visual and literary arts.

Association of Fundraising Consultants (AFC)
The AFC is a UK professional body for fundraising consultants. Founded in 1990 to provide a Europe-wide professional standard in fundraising, the AFC represents the larger UK fundraising consultancies.

CFRE
CFRE is an international body for fundraising professionals, based in Virginia in the USA, which has both individual and organisational members. Founded in 2001, it now has branches in a number of Commonwealth and foreign countries, including the UK. CFRE's Certified Fundraising Executive qualification first became available to British fundraising professionals in 2004.

Community Foundation Network (UKCF)
The UKCF is the umbrella organisation for all community foundations. It provides philanthropic advice to donors, and works to deliver UK-wide fundraising and grant-making programmes through community foundations. There are 46 Community Foundations in the UK, covering all of Scotland, Wales and Northern Ireland; and most of England.

Council for Voluntary Service (CVS)

CVS is a type of local or regional charity in England which provides a variety of services for local voluntary organisations, including advice and training. The umbrella organisation for CVS is the National Association for Voluntary and Community Action (NACVA). In Wales the CVS is called the Community Voluntary Council (CVC). Each county has its own CVC. The equivalents in Scotland and Northern Ireland are the Scottish Council of Voluntary Organisations (SCVO) and the Northern Ireland Council for Voluntary Action (NICVA).

Foundation for Social Improvement (FSI)

Founded by Emma Harrison in 2007, the FSI provides guidance and advice for small charities to enable them to continue providing support for individuals, families, communities and other causes.

Fundraising Standards Board (FRSB)

The FRSB is the only independent self-regulator for fundraising in the UK. It provides a wealth of information and advice to charities and to fundraising suppliers. This includes:

- Supporting charities in complying with fundraising best practice;
- Helping charities identify areas for improvement in their fundraising;
- Ensuring charities are accountable;
- Dealing with charities' concerns and supporting them in handling complaints.

To benefit fully from the FRSB's services, charities need to become members. An annual membership fee is payable.

Heritage Alliance

The Heritage Alliance is the biggest alliance of heritage interests in the UK. It was set up in 2002 to promote the central role of the independent movement in the heritage sector. It provides knowledge and advice on heritage matters, and works to improve public understanding of heritage issues.

Institute of Fundraising (IoF)

The IoF is the largest professional body in fundraising in the UK. Founded in 1983, it now has over 5,300 individual members and 340 organisational members. Although primarily the professional body for fundraisers and fundraising consultants, it provides invaluable services for charities through its groundbreaking Codes of Practice. The IoF has introduced wide-ranging training for fundraising professionals, and has improved professional standards and provided credibility for the profession through the introduction of fundraising qualifications. It works to ensure the highest standards of fundraising practice amongst its members. The IoF website provides very valuable resources and information for small charities.

National Council for Voluntary Organisations (NCVO)

The NCVO is the largest umbrella organisation for the voluntary sector in England. It provides free information, signposting and services both for charities and other voluntary sector organisations and for individual trustees, staff and volunteers.

Small Charities Coalition

The Coalition provides a networking, mentoring and support organisation for small charities. Founded in 2008, it merged with the Charity Trustee Network (CTN) in 2011.

Sports Councils

There is one national sport council – UK Sports Council (UKSC) – and individual sports councils for England, Scotland, Wales and Northern Ireland. UKSC is primarily responsible for elite athletics, whilst the 4 national sport councils seek to encourage mass participation in sport.

Books/pamphlets

Capital Fundraising in the UK – the Compton Way: by Andrew Day and Paul Molloy. Compton International Group Ltd. ISBN: 0-9547519-0-6

City Livery Companies: City of London Public Relations Office.

Complete Fundraising Handbook: by Nina Botting and Michael Norman. Directory of Social Change. ISBN: 1-900360-84-5

Craigmyle Guide to Charitable Giving and Taxation: Craigmyle & Co Ltd.

Directory of Grant Making Trusts: ed. Tom Traynor et al. Directory of Social Change. ISBN: 978-1-903991-79-4

Fundraising for Dummies: by John Mutz and Katherine Murray. Wiley Publishing. ISBN: 978-0-470-56840-8

Fundraising from Europe: by Christopher Carnie. Chapel & York. ISBN: 1-903293-08-1

Fundraising Management – Analysis, planning and practice: by Adrian Sargeant and Elaine Jay. Routledge. ISBN: 978-0-415-45154-3

Guide to the Major Trusts Volumes 1 (The top 400 trusts): by Tom Traynor and Denise Lillya. Directory of Social Change. ISBN: 13-978-1-903991-77-0

Guide to the Major Trusts Volume 2 (the next 1200 trusts): by Alan French and John Smyth. Directory of Social Change. ISBN: 13-978-1-903991-78-7

Guide to UK Company Giving: by John Smith. Directory of Social Change. ISBN: 13-978-1-903991-76-3

Legacy Fundraising – the art of seeking bequests: ed. Sebastian Wilberforce. Directory of Social Change. ISBN: 1-900360-93-4

Tried and Tested Ideas for Raising Money Locally: by Sarah Passingham. Directory of Social Change. ISBN: 13-978-1-903991-37-4

Organising Special Events: Stephen Elsden and John Gray. Directory of Social Change. ISBN: 13-978-1-900360-56-2.

Websites

Association of Charity Fundraising Consultants
www.afc.org.uk

Charities Act 2011
www.legislation.gov.uk/ukpga/2011/25

Charities Aid Foundation
www.cafonline.org

Charity Commission for England and Wales
www.charitycommission.gov.uk

Charity Commission for Northern Ireland
www.charitycommissionni.org.uk

Charity Trustee Network
www.trusteenet.org.uk

CFRE International
www.cfre.org

Community Foundation Network
www.ukcommunityfoundations.org

Company giving information
www.companygiving.org.uk

Entrust (for Landfill Communities Fund)
www.entrust.org.uk

European Funding Office
www.ec.europa.eu

Foundation for Social Improvement
www.thefsi.org

Fundraising Standards Board
www.frsb.org.uk

Giveacar scheme
www.giveacar.co.uk

Government funding information
www.governmentfunding.org.uk

Hemscott Company Guru
www.hemscott.com/guru

HMRC
www.hmrc.gov.uk/charities

Heritage Alliance
www.theheritagealliance.org.uk

Institute of Fundraising
www.institute-of-fundraising.org.uk

JustGiving
www.justgiving.com

Kompass on-line business database
www.kompassinfo.co.uk

MyDonate
www.btplc.com/mydonate

NACVA
www.navca.org.uk

NCVO
www.ncvo.org.uk

NCVO Funding Central
www.fundingcentral.org.uk

National Lottery
www.lotterygoodcauses.org.uk/funding-finder

NICVA
www.nicva.org

Office of the Scottish Charity Regulator
www.oscr.org.uk

Peoplefund.it
www.crowdfunder.co.uk/peoplefundit

SCVO
www.scvo.org.uk

Small Charities Coalition
www.smallcharities.org.uk

Sunday Times Rich List
www.timesplus.co.uk

Trust funding information
www.trustfunding.org.uk

Trustees Unlimited
www.trustees-unlimited.co.uk

Worshipful Company of Fishmongers (for City Livery Companies Directory)
www.fishhall.org.uk

Index

Advance Information Documents (AID) *see* Special Prospects
    Documents
Aggregates Levy Sustainability Fund 107
AID *see* Advance Information Document
Amazon 86

Benedict, Prior 33–5
Birmingham Post's 'Midlands' Rich List', *The* 125
Blue Book, The 125
Bmycharity 180
Board members *see* trustees
Business Plan 35–6, 42–5, 46–9

Campaign Management Team (CMT) 39, 44, 50, 52–9, 70, 129,
    172, 189, 191
    composition 50–2
    office 40–1
    organisation 70
    Secretary 39, 40, 44, 54, 64, 66, 70, 130, 147
        job description 54
    strategy 71
    taskforces 39
    Terms of Reference 52–3
    timetable 67
CASC *see* Community Amateur Sports Club
Case for Support 41
Case Statement 41–3, 44, 57–9, 69
CFT *see* Community Fundraising Team
Chamber of Commerce and Industry 118
Charitable Incorporated Organisation (CIO) 27–8
Charitable Uses, Statute of 25, 28
charity

Acts 26
annual reports 35, 44, 74
business plan 35–6, 42–5, 46–9
Commission for England and Wales 26, 28, 87, 203
Commission for Northern Ireland 26, 28, 203
excepted 29, 36, 150
exempt 29, 150
origins 25
registration 26–8
Church Times 158
CIO *see* Charitable Incorporated Organisation
City of London Livery Companies 85–6
CLG *see* Company Limited by Guarantee
CMT *see* Campaign Management Team
Community Amateur Sports Club (CASC) 27
companies 65
Company donors *see* corporate donors
Company Limited by Guarantee (CLG) 27
corporate donors 115–21
Charity of the Year 119
gifts, cash 116
gifts, in kind 117
sponsorship 115–17

Debrett's *Distinguished People of Today* 125
Directors *see* trustees
Directory of Grant Making Trusts (DGMT) 63, 86, 88, 90, 94
Directory of Social Change 86

EBs *see* Environmental Bodies
Environmental Bodies (EBs) 106
European Union funding 101, 110–12
European Regional Development Fund (ERDF) 111
European Social Fund (ESF) 111
Evening Standard London's 1,000 Most Influential People, *The*
125

financial programme 42–5, 48, 61
foundations *see* trusts and foundations
FRSB *see* Fundraising Standards Board
fundraising
    campaign 33
    capital 37–8
    community 63, 171–85
        auctions 178
        challenge events 181
        community activities 175–6
        Community Fundraising Team (CFT) 172–3
        crowdfunding 182
        events 173–4
        lotteries and raffles 176–8
        on-line 180–1
        recycling 178–9
        sales 174–5
        street collections 176
    constituency 34
    Finale Event 193–4
    leadership 34
    principles 34
    programme 61–2
    project 36–8
    revenue 37
Fundraising Standards Board (FRSB) 43, 200, 204
Funds from Europe *see* European Union funding

Gambling Commission 177
Gift Aid *see* tax efficient giving
Governing Document 30
governors *see* trustees
Grant Making Trusts *see* trusts and foundations
Guardian Media 100', 'The 125
Guide to the Major Trusts 87, 202

Hemscott Company Guru 125, 204
High Sheriff 124, 127
HMRC 81–3, 144, 150, 151, 204

individual donors 64–5, 71, 126, 129–32
    celebrities 123–4
    correspondence 137
    evaluation 126
    'Great & Good' 124–5
    High Net Worth (HNW) 123
    receptions 127, 140–1
    research 124
    training for approaches 133–6
Institute of Fundraising (IoF) 28, 43
    Code of Practice 43
International Authors' and Writers' Who's Who, The 125

JustGiving (Vodafone) 180

Kompass 118, 122, 204

Landfill Communities Fund (LCF) 106
Landfill Operators (LOs) 106–7
Landfill Tax Credit Scheme (LTCS) *see* Landfill Communities
    Fund
LCF *see* Landfill Communities Fund
LOs *see* Landfill Operators
legacies 197–9
Leverhulme, Lord 115
Lieutenancy Office 124
Lions 66, 172
Local Education Authority 76
Local Government Councils 63–4, 102; *see also* statutory fund-
    ing
    empowerment funds 64, 102, 105
    lotteries and raffles 176–8

MyDonate (BT) 180

National Council for Voluntary Organisations (NCVO) 63, 201, 205
National Lottery 71, 108–10, 171
    Big Lottery 71, 108
    demonstrating outcomes 114
    history 108
NCVO *see* National Council for Voluntary Organisations
Nuffield, Lord 115

Office of the Scottish Charity Regulator (OSCR) 26, 28, 29, 63, 87, 90, 205
Office of the Third Sector 87
OSCR *see* Office of the Scottish Charity Regulator

patrons 72, 159, 188
Peterborough Cathedral 33
planning 66
police 173
Presidents *see* patrons
public benefit 28, 41
public relations (PR) 50, 66, 157
    media 159
    newsletters 162
    plan 160
    social media 162
    training 167
    websites 163

recycling 77, 158
research 62, 86, 97, 124
Rotary 66, 172
Round Table 66, 172
Royal British Legion 172

Service Level Agreements (SLAs) 46, 63, 102
SLAs *see* Service Level Agreements
Small and Medium size Enterprises (SMEs) 82, 116, 147, 148
SMEs *see* Small and Medium size Enterprises
Special Prospects Documents 39, 189–90
Sportsmatch 120
statutory funding 104
   demonstrating outcomes 114
   local government 104
   national government 103
   National Health Service (NHS) 102
Sunday Times Rich List 64, 125
support material 187
   campaign brochures 189
   campaign leaflets 188
   DVDs 190
   souvenirs 191
   Special Prospects Documents (SPD) 189

taskforces *see* Campaign Management Team
tax efficient giving 75, 144
   assets, gifts of 146
   corporation tax 75, 79, 146
   covenants 145
   Gift Aid 143
      Gift Aid Certificate 152
      Gift Aid Small Donations Scheme (GASDS) 144
   gifts, in kind 147
   inheritance tax 75, 147
   payroll giving 147
   shares, gifts of 146
training 66, 133, 167
trust fundraising 67, 86
trustees
   appointment before registering charity 31
   recruitment 31

skills required 31
trusts and foundations 85
    research 85

VAT 149
Virgin Money Giving 180
volunteers
    general 34
    leaders 34
    trustees 31, 36

websites 87, 169
Who's Who? 125
Women's Institute 172

NELL JAMES PUBLISHERS
www.nelljames.co.uk

250+ fundraising ideas for your charity, society, school and PTA
by Paige Robinson

How to overcome fear of driving
The road to driving confidence
by Joanne Mallon

Blogging for happiness
A guide to improving positive mental health (and wealth) from your blog
by Ellen Arnison

Birth trauma: A guide for you, your friends and family to coping with post-traumatic stress disorder following birth
by Kim Thomas

Survival guide for new parents
Pregnancy, birth and the first year
by Charlie Wilson

Toddlers: an instruction manual
A guide to surviving the years one to four (written by parents, for parents)
by Joanne Mallon

Test tubes and testosterone
A man's journey into infertility and IVF
by Michael Saunders

Lightning Source UK Ltd.
Milton Keynes UK
UKOW04f0946300715

256092UK00001B/11/P